The Great Ap

Life in the Cult of Jeho

CW01500991

by Neil Gardner

Acknowledgements

This book has taken a long time to write. It would never have happened without the support of my wife Lynda and my children Daniel and Emily.

Lynda, you are the lynchpin of our family and without you we are just a group of random idiots.

Thanks too to the Vast Apostate Army, you have been true friends and I love you all.

More thanks to Rohan who has helped me many times, you know what you did.

Thank you to all the people who watch and comment on my YouTube channel "The Great Apostate".

Finally thanks to you! For buying this book! I hope it helps everyone who reads it.

This is the story of my life as a member of the cult known as Jehovah's Witnesses. As it is my story it also includes details of my family members, old friends and people I used to know. Where I felt it was necessary I used a pseudonym to replace the real peoples names. This is **MY** story and **MY** memory, no one else's and although some details may not be perfect I'm at least seventy percent happy that they are. If you think your are mentioned in this book, you're not and if you think it happened a different way, go write your own book!

This book was never intended to give readers a step by step explanation about what is wrong with my old cult, there are lot's of books out there that do that and in fact do it better than I could do. This book is about my life inside a cult and the how that affected me. It gives you a tiny glimpse into day to day cult activities and shows you what tricks they use to keep members. For the sake of clarity, I have added a list of the very best places to learn about the Jehovah's Witnesses biggest errors and lies.

If you want to read a book that details exactly what is wrong with the Jehovah's Witnesses then I can help you. That book was written by the late Ray Franz and it was called *Crisis of Conscience*. He was a member of the Governing Body of Jehovah's Witnesses and left after realizing he could no longer be a part of such a destructive cult. The book is out of print at the moment but a quick web search will lead you to a PDF of it.

If you want a STEP BY STEP guide on HOW to leave the Jehovah's Witnesses I can also help! That book was written by me and is called *How to Leave a Cult*. It's available on Amazon in paperback or digitally, I hear it's awesome!

I know what you you're thinking "Why should I read another book by a disgruntled (funny word that) EX Jehovah's Witnesses and what is so special about your book to make it worth my valuable time?" Well I could explain to you why this book is awesome but why do that when I can use the words of famous Jehovah's Witnesses from the past to do it for me!

Charles Taze Russell

(Founder of The International Bible Students which would later become the Jehovah's Witnesses)

"Who'd have thought that just over a century after my death someone would come along with the wisdom of Solomon and the wit of Mark Twain? I cannot thank Neil enough for bringing to light this tale of life inside the religion I founded so long ago. Now you might know that I like to dabble in predicting things, I have in fact predicted the end of the world on many occasions but even I was unable to predict this books extraordinary success. If only I had looked deeper in the great pyramid of Giza!"

Joseph (Judge) Rutherford

(Second leader of The International Bible Students)

"Hic.....somebody get me another bottle of whisky!" what? this things on? DAMMIT Jane!"

"Hello I'm Joseph Rutherford and Neil asked me to write a forward to his book about my, I mean Jehovah gods, religion. He is very wise to concentrate on this magnificent religion, after all, where else will you find all my many many book and pamphlets?"

"What? they don't study my books any more?"

"New Light?"

"They don't even mention me any more!"

"I made those people what they are! Without me they're just a bunch of crazies who study pyramids! Showwww me the way to go hooomm-meee, I'm tired and I wanna go to zzzzzzzz. Bring me another bottle."

"Oh yeah, read Neil's book."

Raymond Franz

(Former Member Of The Governing Body Of Jehovah's Witnesses and The ACTUAL Great Apostate)

"When I left the Jehovah's Witnesses and wrote *Crisis Of Conscience*, I had no idea that Neil and his family were still going to the meetings only a few hundred miles away from me. If I had known that he go on to write this after reading my book, I might have ditched the whole idea completely. I mean how does he think I'm going to recommend this book? I'm a deeply religious man and he's clearly a terrible human being. If you want to read his book I can only have pity on you."

Well, with those less than heartfelt recommendations let's get started with my book!

Introduction

I remember the first time I was really truly terrified. It was at the RDS Convention Centre in Dublin Ireland, I was about eight years old and walking hand in hand with my dad, David "Leslie" Gardner. We were enjoying a break in the proceedings during the four day District Assembly.

"Dad, what will you do when they come and take us away?" I asked quietly. My dad paused and said "Oh, It'll be OK Neil don't worry so much" my dad was never one to go into existential angst too deeply!

Though he had tried to calm my fears it wasn't enough and this was the first of many times in my childhood that I would fixate about religiously motivated, satanically inspired government agents removing me from the arms of my parents.

I had just spent the morning sitting quietly in my suit listening to a talk form the platform, from there the speaker told us all horrific tales about how children in my religion had been snatched from their families by the Nazi's during World War Two. The Nazi's had decided that they could do a better job of raising them and so they were taken by force. This was not just the actions of a tyrannical government, oh no! You see the Nazi's were inspired to take those kids by none other than Satan The Devil, the ruler of this world and everyone in it!

So, this was why an eight year old kid worried about being taken from his parents in the dead of night by evil social workers. When other kids were learning to do stunts on their skateboards, I fascinated by the end of the world, or "Armageddon" as I was taught to call it.

We were told, on that day, and throughout my childhood from various platforms, magazines and books that this would happen again soon and

5

as children we had to make our faith strong, you know, for when we were living in a group home and denied even our Bibles!

I was born into a small religious cult known as the Jehovah's Witnesses and this cult took over every moment of my, and my families lives from about two years before my birth until I reached the age of twenty five and finally made the break with my old cult and started living.

As a nipper I had been taught that the end of "This Wicked System Of Things" was very very near. I had enjoyed a constant diet of bad news and propaganda, all aimed at convincing me, no convincing is the wrong word, indoctrinating me, better yet, brainwashing me, all to believe that I was part of a small selected group of people who, with hard work and a little luck (not that I believed in luck!) would make it through this global apocalypse and "Live Forever In A Paradise Earth".

As a Jehovah's Witness my whole life revolved around "The Truth" and the "Kingdom Hall", our church. Everything I did or thought, every plan or purchase was filtered through my "Witness" software. Unlike most Christian denominations my moral compass wasn't "What Would Jesus Do" it was "What Will The Brothers Think" and nothing in life was small enough to ignore this Jehovah's Witness prime directive.

Toys, books, movies and clothes, all these things were subject to strict policing to make sure I did not fall foul of congregational discipline or my own warped guilty conscience.

What I studied at school or whether I took on extra curricular activities, indeed, how long I was even allowed to go to school or what I studied would all be decided by a rigid application of the religious teachings found only in Jehovah's Witness publications. The ultimate example of this was the "Watchtower" magazine! Published every two weeks and full to the brim with all the teachings of Jehovah God no less! Deliv-

ered straight to you, from Gods lips to your ears and only partially filtered by the leaders of my cult "The Governing Body Of Jehovah's Witnesses".

These exalted men were part of an elite and selected group of men,
women too but we'll get to that later as only men can serve on the governing body. They had been chosen by the creator of the universe himself (He is definitely by the way!). Their role was to provide "Food At
The Proper Time" specifically for us, the only members of Gods true
religion. More generally, they were also a huge shining lighthouse for
the peoples of the world, warning them that they were headed to dangerous and deadly rocks and that Satan was ruling this corrupted earth
and they needed to "Flee To Safety" safety only found within the arms
of my cult. Some will take offence at my use of the word "Cult" I know,
it hurts your feelings and you're NOT a cult, well you ARE and it's my
book, if it hurts your feelings, write your own book!

When Frank McCourt wrote his Pulitzer Prize winning *Angela's Ashes*
an epic story of growing up a poor Catholic in Limerick, it ruffled more
than a few feathers and led to the publication of a "counter" to his
book. It claimed to offer an alternative view from the eyes of people
who "had the courage to stick it out" and though it was largely rubbish,
I applaud the effort. If after reading this book you feel angry or think I
am lying I invite you to get your laptop out and start typing!

I know what you're thinking "Boo Hoo, another misery memoir from
someone who can't get over the past" and in some ways you'd be right!
This is a memoir about my life inside a cult, how it worked, what was
wrong about it and how it affected me and those I love. I'd be lying if I
said that it is easy to "Get over" the past, the past has long tentacles and
doesn't let go quickly or easily. Even when it is far behind you in the
mirror it has a habit of jumping back in front of you and forcing you to
deal with it all over again, but enough of these mixed metaphors!

So yes, this is a misery memoir and no, I didn't get over it! not completely, but I hope that by telling my story, I can help you understand what happens in a cult, how it catches its victims and why they stay a part of it all, even when they finally learn that it's all a big lie.

This book will not just tell you about my own experiences, I also want to let you know a bit about the cult I was a part of for two and half decades. I want you to try to see it as I saw it, nearly perfect. I want you to try and figure out how a person can hold that view, while at the same time enduring injustice and being unjust to those around you.

How bad does a religion need to be to turn you into the very worst version of YOU you could ever hope to be? A person who is incapable of keeping a secret or of being trusted, who could look at their parents, even their own children and cut them off for the rest of their lives? It seems incredible to me looking back on it, but being a member of the Jehovah's Witnesses made the sort of people that could look at a victim of child sex abuse and make the conscious decision to stand with the abuser instead. We certainly were a calculating bunch!

I now view my time in a cult with so much regret. It harmed me and my family so very much and some of that harm can never be undone. Yet my family went along with much of it, convinced that we were serving Jehovah and that we must serve him above all else. It was this very sincerity and dedication that meant we were most harmed by the false teachings we considered true.

I hope that my story will help current members to escape from the Jehovah's Witnesses as I did. I hope it allows them to start to see through the lie that they have believed for so long, a lie that promises "Brotherhood" but instead offers captivity. Promises of life long relationships and claims that its members are "The Happiest people On Earth" but instead saddles them with conditional "Strings Attached" relationships and a good chance of a lifelong mental illness.

It is my deepest wish that this book makes you laugh too, as the situations and experiences that a dedicated cult member can find themselves in are often bizarre! This book will, I hope, open your mind and allow you to avoid making the same mistakes I did.

Even though I am now that I am out in "The World", as Jehovah's Witnesses call it, I see the same type of mistakes being made by people of all faiths and maybe this book along, with the other types of activism I have taken part in, will stop you wasting your lives and the lives of your children.

Another Fine Mess You Got Us Into!

So, how does a nice family from Northern Ireland end up in a cult? For that answer you'll have to ask the people responsible, my parents. Thankfully, they are both still alive and able to tell me what you need to know. I am further blessed by the fact that my mum and dad left my cult, the Jehovah's Witnesses about eighteen months after I did and it's for that reason that we are allowed to talk to one another.

What do you mean, "allowed to talk to one another"? Well, I'm glad you asked! You are clearly a smart reader! You see the Jehovah's Witnesses, like many other cults practice "Shunning". This means that if a member is naughty and gets expelled, or even just gets a bit bored and wanders off the reservation they are officially or unofficially "Shunned". Their friends and family are ordered to stop having anything to do with them, refuse to eat with them or even say hello if they pass on the street! If they don't want to do that then THEY will be disfellowshipped and find themselves in exactly the same position.

I remember one Jehovah's Witness friend talking to my brother a few years before we left. He had just had his first child, a boy and was holding him in his arms.

"He beautiful isn't he Steven" the man said my brother replied that, yes, indeed he was a lovely baby. "But If he ever leaves Jehovah he's dead to me" the new dad said emphatically. I think this event alone was one of those that made us both question our choice of religion.

I'd like to tell you that this attitude was rare, but I'd be lying, in fact it was that very attitude that years before had led me and my family to abandon almost all contact with my own sister and shun her for twelve long years, but more of that later.

10

My parents have been able to talk to me about what brought them into
what would always and forever be known to us as "The Truth". Settle
down because we are about to begin a story exactly like 7 million others. A story of loss, sadness and loneliness involving a very nice Eng-
lish couple who entered my parents lives and introduced them to "Love
Bombing" and so much other nonsense. It all seemed so sensible at the
time.

We flash back to 1972 when people still felt bad about the Beatles split-
ting up and when British cars were still terrible but they were all we
had. There was no internet or mobile phones and household phone
lines were only installed if you had a really good reason for getting one.
"Made In China" printed on something was a sure-fire promise that it
was crap whereas "Made In Britain" was a promise that it had taken two
years longer than necessary, due to strikes, and it would begin to rust
the instant you took it out of the shop.

It was in those days that my mum and dad, Rosemary and Leslie Gardner were living in a fairly new government built housing estate in
Antrim a few miles outside Belfast. They had moved their so my dad
could start work in a new factory that had just opened and though they
had to move away from where they grew up in Belfast this job promised
to more than double what my dad had made as Postman. They already
had two kids by then, my Sister Karen and my brother Steven. My mum
had recently lost her dad to a heart attack.

George Keel was a nice, if easy to anger father. My mother loved him
and still talks about him often. He had served in the Royal Air Force
during World War Two and fought throughout the war in Europe. He
came home with what people would now call Post Traumatic Stress
Disorder and never fully recovered from it. He was, in many ways, my
mums moral compass and it was obvious that she looked up to him. So
when he died in his early sixties it came as a huge shock to her and she

was grief stricken and depressed and the fact that she was miles away from her mother Mary Keel made this even worse.

My father had just said goodbye to his entire family who had immigrated to Canada. His identical twin brother Charles had gone a few years earlier and mum and dad were left alone raising a young family. It would be safe to say that our little family were easy pickings for the Jehovah's Witnesses. All they needed to do was show us a bit of love and attention and we would get swept along with it and into the waiting arms of a cult!.

It was then that a couple of Jehovah's Witnesses found their way, Frank and Sally Madorski. They had been working on the "Door To Door Ministry Work" and spent their lives doing this working as "Pioneers". Pioneers are special Jehovah's Witnesses, they have given up hope of "Worldly Riches" and sacrificed their own hopes and dreams. These were replaced with a promise to spend as much time as they humanly could preaching to everyone they saw about the awesome prize available to faithful Jehovah's Witnesses, maybe, if you did everything you were told.

My mum and dad didn't automatically rush off to join the Jehovah's Witnesses, instead they had a friendly relationship with Frank and Sally but didn't even bother going to the meetings at the local Kingdom Hall. My mum told me of the times when they weren't in the mood for a conversation about religion and so they hid quietly until Frank and Sally had stopped knocking and left.

A few years later my father got the chance to move to a new start-up company called Grundig. They were opening in the town of Lisburn, about twelve miles away, and after a brief interview the young Gardner clan packed up once more and moved to another new Council run housing estate called "Hill Hall". When they left they had no plans to continue hanging out with Jehovah's Witnesses but it wasn't to be because although mum and dad were planning on forgetting about them, the Jehovah's Witnesses had not forgotten about mum and dad.

I wasn't born yet but somehow mum and dad were settling into life in Lisburn without me. Steven was only a baby and Karen had started at Largymore Primary School just up the road. Life was good but my parents were still lonely and missing their families very much. My mum still had her mother, though the short distance from Belfast made seeing her a little harder than it needed to be. It was then that my dad met and made friends with a man called Peter Hill. Peter was a co-worker of my dads and by all accounts a pretty decent straight shooting guy, it was of course a complete coincidence that Peter and his wife Cicely were also Pioneers for the Jehovah's Witnesses!.

How did a tiny cult with less then three thousand members in my country manage to keep popping in and out of my parents life you ask? Well it was easy, the Jehovah's Witnesses were and remain, excellent record keepers! Every interaction with a "Worldly" person was recorded and handed in to the congregation secretary, a Senior man who served as a leader. They were particularly interested in how long a Witness spent preaching to them and these records also included your address, details about your family and what tricks had already been used on you with or without success.

It is likely that my parents passed on the approximate area they were moving to when they left Antrim and this information was passed on down the road to the next pioneer who could introduce themselves and start the sales pitch all over again. The Jehovah's Witnesses play the long game and unless you expressly say you aren't interested and never will be, you will never be done with them.

It wasn't long before Peter and Cicely had started a Bible study with my parents. That led to them being introduced to other Jehovah's Witness families living nearby and these families soon became friends. At the same time mum and dad were very subtly being brainwashed. They were told that what they were learning was unique and if they left they couldn't get it anywhere else and as my father was the head of a household he would be responsible before God Jehovah for the fate and certain deaths of his children on Gods day of judgement at Armageddon, which really was any day now!.

They were also told that "The whole world is lying in the power of the wicked one" namely Satan The Devil and "No matter who it was or how small a matter it might be, things were all following his evil plan" which was to separate you from this wonderful new truth.

"Your family will try to make you stop studying" they said "They'll say we're a cult. Do we LOOK like a cult?". They also promised a reward to those who remained faithful, life eternal on a paradise earth! You might also see your dead relatives and friends. What a wonderful promise this was for my mum who was still missing her father!.

Adding to this old fashioned brainwashing was the fact that my parents were on their own and the Jehovah's Witnesses seemed so NICE! They smiled and were happy, they always asked how you were doing and at a time in my country when Catholics and Protestants were killing each other in record numbers they were an outstanding example of "Christian Neutrality". Former Catholics, with a history of terrorist violence, stood side by side with Protestant former soldiers and sang from the "Kingdom Melodies" songbook! It really looked like a true brotherhood, a paradise on earth.

It was all these things and more that helped convince my mum and later my dad to get baptized and become Jehovah's Witnesses. They were convinced that this was a wise and sound choice for their family and that only good could come from it, sadly they were very wrong.

Lisburn is a nice place, I'm still here all these years later so it must be! There are lots of shops, it's close to everything, jobs are fairly plentiful and taxes are low, so If you want my opinion, I'm a fan. It was into this town, albeit a lot smaller back then, that I was born on the 5th of November 1974. I like to think that my brother and sister were just some less than satisfactory practice runs that led up to me, but as Steven loves to tell me, "You are the accident". I remember when he said this the first time I was horrified and ran to my mum and dad, "Mum, Steven said I'm an accident" I whined, "No Neil, not at all" mum replied. "You were, um, a delightful surprise!"

Let's set aside my standing as planned or unplanned for the moment. Whatever the answer I can tell you that I was welcomed into a warm and loving home and was lucky to be there. If only the story ended here! if only I went on to have loving parents and sarcastic siblings. Maybe then I'd have had a normal everyday life but that was not to be because I was born into this faith, my own personal cult and I was about to experience twenty five years of near constant nonsense until I finally had enough and gave up.

Being born a Jehovah's Witness is pretty much the same as being born into any other cult or religion, so long as you and mum survive the birth. Since Jehovah's Witnesses are taught, well let's be honest ordered, to avoid blood at any cost, a steady stream of mothers and babies have died over the decades because they refused blood transfusions. Luckily, I made it out alive and returned home to Hill Hall Estate to start my life!

Lisburn Kingdom Hall was a pretty standoffish place but my mum and dad made it work. I have asked for stories about those days and my dad was very clear about wanting me to tell you about the time he needed a motorbike to drive to work. Witnesses try to stay away from dealing with "Worldly" people as they call them so dad was happy when one of the local "Elders" told him he had a lovely motorbike he could have cheap.

Elders are the leaders of a Jehovah's Witness Kingdom Hall. They run the show, usually as part of a "Body" of Elders which can be anything from one overworked guy to a dozen or more who break up the responsibilities between them all. This Elder, let's call him Moses, was kind enough to come to my dad and take the money first because he was just that kind of guy! He would then return with the motorbike. My dads face must have been a picture when the bike was delivered, dumped really, off the back of a trailer, It's engine didn't start because it was rusted solid!

This was just the beginning of my families dealings with "Jehovah's People". Witnesses are taught that they are exceptional people who are the most trustworthy and honest to be found anywhere but a closer examination reveals that every type of crime imaginable is committed inside the secure walls of those Kingdom Halls.

So you've just seen with your own eyes that life in "The Truth", as all Jehovah's Witnesses call it, is very far from perfect why stick around? Well, it's complicated but I'll try to explain. As you get deeper and deeper into a cult you are taught that the people who love you, family and friends who are not in the cult are out to spoil things for you.

They are working to destroy your faith and get you away from the wonderful things you have learned only to make you "return to the same low sink of debauchery" as they are in! With ideas like this in your head, you can start to see why cult members are reluctant to leave the fold of a group that they have come to trust above all else, even their own parents!

You also have to bare in mind that the leaders of cults will also tell you that any problems you see within the group are YOUR fault, or are the consequence of sin. These problems will be solved by Jehovah in his due time and if you want it dealt with faster it says more about you than it does about the problems! You are told to "Wait on Jehovah" and then move on. If you can't do that well, they have ways of making you not talk!

Jehovah's Witnesses are further instructed that going to the "The World" about internal problems will "bring reproach upon Jehovah's name" and so if you are sold a broken motorbike by a scumbag car salesman who values cash over the well being of a young family, you'd better suck it up and forget about it!

Around the time little Neil reached eighteen months my family had a bit of bad luck. We were living through what was known as "The Troubles" and you probably know Irish Republicans were fighting a quasi civil war against the British Government in an effort to restore a United Ireland. In response to this "Loyalist" terrorists rose up. They claimed to be fighting back against the Irish Republican Army and protecting loyal Protestants.

As is usually the case with things like this, both sides spent a lot of time committing terrible crimes and one particular crime involved accidentally throwing a bomb through my parents front window. Mum and dad were not in at the time, neither were Steven or Karen but I'm pleased to say both my grandmother and I were. Once the fire brigade lifted the remains of our house off our heads both of us were fine, though this did become the catalyst for my families next big move. To Canada and beyond, well just to Canada.

My whole family stood shivering outside Pearson International Airport in Toronto Canada. We'd arrived in the middle of a freezing minus thirty Canadian winter wearing clothes that were only suitable for zero degrees Celsius. All our worldly belongings were beside us in a few small suitcases, it was a truly pitiful site. My grandfather picked us up and deposited us at my uncles house, who had kindly paid for our flights there.

To say my grandfather was not nice would be an understatement. He was rude, mean and a bully but worst of all he very obviously didn't care about my dad or his family. Dad was and is still a very mild mannered man and was never able to stand up for himself and "Grumpa" as my brother Steven christened him, was not interested in helping us settle at all.

We stayed with my Uncle Charles for several months, but he was in the middle of his first bad marriage and the entire situation was never going to work out. Dad quickly got work and we were able to move to the city of Leamington, near the border with the USA. Even then, mum and dad were not totally sold on the idea of finding a Kingdom Hall and going to the meetings. Once again, the Jehovah's Witnesses found us and due to our crappy extended family situation, we welcomed all the help we could get. Even now, decades later, my parents speak of the help they received in those days as lifesaving and although I have much to criticise the Jehovah's Witnesses for, I can't fault how we were treated during the years we spent in Canada.

Of course, I was a child and had a child's understanding of what was going on around me. There is no doubt that all manner of nastiness was hiding in the shadows, but as a child I had no complaints. At one point during our stay in Canada there was a major chemical spill nearby and tens of thousands of people had to evacuate. My extended family all left to go to wherever they felt was safe but they didn't feel inclined to offer us any help. I still remember my parents driving up to the grounds of a dedicated Assembly Hall run by the Witnesses in the dead of night to ask for help.

The custodian and his wife took us in immediately. They fed us and put us up for several nights in the sick bay on tiny cots until it was safe to return home, so credit where it's due, some Jehovah's Witnesses were good people. It turned out both he and his wife were also musicians who wrote many of the songs we knew by heart in our version of a hymn book "Sing Praises To Jehovah" and we had a very nice time singing them together and playing in a huge empty stadium.

I have asked my parents if they have any comments or complaints about the Witnesses during our time in Canada and they can't think of any. They did say that people took the cult much more seriously there than back in Northern Ireland meaning "If you screw up you will get in a lot more trouble". Of course ALL Jehovah's Witnesses share the same beliefs and so if you get into trouble in one country the system for punishing you will be the same. The same rules will apply to refusing blood transfusions or leaving school early to become a pioneer as they do toward child sexual abuse. Rules that allow child abusers to hide out so easily within the Kingdom Hall and actively punish families who come forward to report sex crimes but we weren't aware of that happening at the time.

All in all it is safe to say I am fan of Canada. No I LOVE Canada. To this day I bleed maple syrup! And it is with sadness that I now have to tell you about what happened that forced us to leave Canada and return to Lisburn.

We had moved around quite a bit during our time in Canada and ended up in the City of Mississauga. We lived in a rent controlled housing estate called Erin Mills which was built along the Erin Mills Trail, a lovely walkway that I took every weekday to Brookmede Kindergarten. We were very lucky to get in and as my dad is an incredibly likeable guy he was able to help one of his sisters, Betty, and later his mum and dad to move in too. This was not enough to make them treat him any better or pay any attention whatsoever to his children and we continued to rely on the local Jehovah's Witnesses for friendship and support. To show you how useless my grandparents were I will tell you a story.

Picture it, I'm 6 years old and playing in the street. Suddenly I need to poop but my house is to far away! "I know, I'll go to Grandma's" I say! So off I run all the while holding in a poop as only a kid can do. I get to the front door, of the house they only got because my dad is nice, and screamed "Grandma I need to poop, let me in" I waited a full minute and then heard my grandfather say "Don't open it, I don't want him in" heartbroken and full to the brim of poop I ran as fast as could to get home and almost made but I didn't. If there was a hell my grandfather would be there, he was a dirtbag and I don't miss him one bit.

In happier news my dad had found an excellent job working for an electronics company that built guidance systems and he quickly became a supervisor. Things were looking up! Then they started looking down again. Dad's company was awarded the contract to build the guidance systems for the new "Cruise Missiles". This would give him a big bump in pay and years of security, including awesome benefits for his family but that wasn't enough of a reason for him to stay, in fact nothing could make him stay because he wasn't allowed to!

Jehovah's Witnesses claim to be neutral (although they aren't) and they are not allowed to be members of the police or military so my dad helping to build the most accurate killing machines ever invented was bound to ruffle a few feathers! So as good Jehovah's Witnesses mum and dad went to the Elders to ask them what they needed to do.

"Quit your job" they said.

"Jehovah will provide" they said.

"He looks after the birds doesn't he?" they said.

"Yes but my kids can't eat bugs!" mum replied.

"QUIT YOUR JOB OR ELSE" they commanded. "Jehovah will kill you and your children at Armageddon, which is coming VERY soon" they told my parents.

If dad stayed in his job he would be at risk of being "Disfellowshipped" or shunned. All the friendship and support we had gotten from the brother and sisters within the hall would end immediately, the love tap would be turned off and we would be left to fend for ourselves, strangers in a strange land. Against this threat we were powerless and my dad put in his resignation letter.

As luck would have it, Jehovah did provide. Sadly he does not pay as well as a weapons manufacturer and the new jobs benefits sucked. Dad ended up earning a lot less and having to travel further to work so we saw him a lot less, then our own personal Armageddon actually did happen.

Dad was working with a large machine which pressed computer chips into circuit boards and making sure that they were aligned. He saw that one chip had been misplaced and quickly reached in to reposition it before a heavy steel press pushed them into place. That was the day my dad learned the hard way why he wasn't supposed to wear a watch on the shop floor.

He replaced the computer chip easily enough but as he removed his hand the two tonne press began swinging towards him, this was when his watch strap became caught on a piece of metal and held his hand fast. Dad has talked to me about what happened a few times, it usually boils down to him staring wildly as the machines press got ever closer, him gritting his teeth and then watching horrified as two tonnes of solid steel neatly severed his left hand. He tells me he's still not sure how he did it but somehow he was able to pull the machine up and remove the mangled hand, no doubt before fainting as he's always been terrified of blood!

Dad was rushed to the hospital and was incredibly lucky to get advanced microsurgery which back then was relatively new. They spent hours reattaching his hand and I'm happy to say they were successful. The next day the surgeon who performed this miracle came to see dad and dad honestly said "Will I be able to play the piano again?" The doctor told him he would and my father uttered those famous words "That's funny, I couldn't before". I'm not saying he invented this joke, but if he didn't he had heard it really, really early and it was still hilarious.

Since dad worked for a small company he got no help whatsoever and our family drifted into debt fast. Dad's family were not much help and my parents began to consider moving back to Northern Ireland. They knew that moving home would be hard, but they also knew that they would get help through state welfare and my other grandmother would be there for us. She was a wonderful lady who came to see us as often as she could and who we ended up living with briefly on the seventh floor in a two bedroom apartment In Belfast.

After six years my family packed our bags, we kids gathered up our toys and headed for the airport. My parents had sold anything they could to get a few dollars together, including their car, so when dad needed to drive somewhere the day before we left he asked Grumpa, as dad was waiting at the front door he heard his father say "The sooner they get away from here and back home the better" Dad turned around and we made do without a car until some local Witnesses loaned him one. Today his final messages, the curse of my asshole grandfather and his loud whispers struck again.

We flew into England and then took the ferry over the Irish Sea into Belfast. I was really excited as I had visited a year earlier and met up with kids my own age. I was certain that I would love living here and even though I had actually been born in Lisburn, it felt like a new world to me. Dad had warned us all that if we returned, we would be heading back to Lisburn to live and the Congregation of Jehovah's Witnesses that lived their had a bad reputation for being weird and standoffish, like a Celtic version of the movie Deliverance!

We stayed in Belfast for a few weeks living in my Grannies flat. I had stayed there a year earlier and been amazed as I watched out the window and stared at a tank driving up the train tracks not far away to inspect a bomb, you might think that kind of thing is terrifying but to a child it was exciting stuff! We moved to Lisburn after a few weeks and moved into 26, Causeway End Park. It was a new council house built on three floors and we felt so lucky to have it. We really felt Jehovah was truly looking out for us but if that were true he would have kept us far from the Jehovah's Witnesses in the first place!

I was now 8 years old and my family started attending Lisburn Kingdom Hall. This was to be the centre of my life for another 17 years. It would be my focus and where I learned everything I considered important. The members of that Hall automatically became my brothers and sisters, the Elders would be my leaders, policemen and Judges. I would have to fit its goals into my dreams and it would shape me and my future. God help me.

A Kid In "The Truth"

There are lots of different kinds of Jehovah's Witness, some are in it because they married a girl who already was, some are in it but aren't really interested and others are only there because the have a fanatical spouse who will make their lives a misery if they stop going. Yet more remain in because they have friends inside and know that if they leave those same friends won't be coming with them and won't ever talk to them again! Then there is a very large group, a group that I was once a very proud member of – The True Believers.

True believers actually lived the life of a Jehovah's Witness as best we could in the way we were ordered to do so. We went to all the meetings, studied beforehand, did personal Bible study and went out on the "Preaching Work". We prayed incessantly and felt never ending guilt if we failed to live up to the impossible and often hypocritical standards we were obliged to adopt. We went to all the Assemblies **and** took notes! We did talks from the platform, even when we were young kids but more important than all this, we got Baptized!

I'm not in any way trying to attack those who made it through their time in the Jehovah's Witnesses in whatever ways they thought best. Though it was often really annoying, when you stood up in class and refused to take part in various "unacceptable" practices, like making Easter or Christmas cards, attending school assemblies or studying other religions only to know that a lot of other Witness kids were hiding the very fact that they WERE witnesses from teachers and classmates alike!

These days I try to think of it like a concentration camp, who am I to judge how you survived? Just because I used one strategy and you used another, I try to be happy that we both got out alive. Alright, a small part of me still thinks you're a dick, but I'm working on it.

A child growing up in the early 1980's was spoiled for fun! It was just long enough ago that our parents allowed us to play outdoors all day and building sites were our play parks! We had the Space Shuttle and awesome cartoons to keep us entertained and video games were just getting good. But for some of us, those things took a back seat. For those of us unlucky enough to be Jehovah's Witness children we had far higher goals, we would forego almost all holidays, because they were either "Satanic" or "Worldly".

Christmas became just another day, although one with good movies on TV! Halloween was evil so most times we would either arrange to be away from home, easy as we spent many nights at the Kingdom Hall, or we would simply hide upstairs with the blinds closed hoping to be left alone. We would scoff at the people who did celebrate these occasions "Don't they know Jesus wasn't born on Christmas day" we'd smugly say. "Halloween is all about devil worship" but one event that we missed that even we couldn't explain was Birthdays!

Birthdays were forbidden in our churches because.......well, just because. They did have a lame excuse that birthdays were only mentioned in the bible in a negative way and so we should have nothing to do with them although nobody was really happy with this teaching we all obeyed while still remaining puzzled by it all. Parents never got the chance to show their cuddly baby during milestone years and children never enjoyed the wonderful feeling of knowing one day a year that was just about them.

The Jehovah's Witnesses continue to forbid celebrating birthdays and still use the same old excuses, but if you ask me they do it to further isolate members and make children outcasts among kids they may meet. I was 30 years old when I celebrated my first birthday and I loved every minute of it, I wish I had been able to enjoy 29 more birthdays a bit sooner!

We were chosen to be "Spiritual Soldiers" not that we'd be getting any cool guns. Instead we were armed with Bibles and a seemingly never ending supply of literature supplied by The Watchtower Bible And Tract Society this is the publishing arm of the Jehovah's Witnesses. With these "Spiritual Weapons" we spent our time going to constant meetings at the Kingdom Hall, out door to door preaching and three weekends a year at Circuit and District assemblies, the typical routine of a Witness in my day went like this -

- First of all we had the Tuesday night book study and the study for the study. Add to this 30 minutes before getting ready and 1hour afterwards and you get, well you get a lot! I make it to be about 2 ½ hours on Tuesday alone!

- Then we move on to Thursday, the big daddy of the week! That's 1 hour 45 mins plus 30 minutes before getting dressed and 1 hour afterwards again (what did we say to each other that we needed to stay so long for?) This gives us another 3 hours and 15 minutes on a school night! While we're at it what kind of parents think its OK to keep their kids out late on a school night TWO TIMES A WEEK EVERY WEEK!?!? Is it any wonder we were all tired, we never went to sleep!

- So far we are at 5 hours 45 minutes a week. But wait...it's not over yet! Any self respecting Jehovah's Witness needs to be out on service on a Friday night and if you're dumb like me you spent the rest of that night studying with friends for the Sunday watchtower! To be fair, I'll only count the time I spent studying that shitty rag and we STILL get another 2 ½ hours on Friday night alone!

• So Saturday comes along and what were you doing? That's right, Service. You can add another 2 hours walking very slowly from one house to the next, 30 minutes getting ready and getting home and you can put another 3 hours to your tally! WOW! So far we have 11 hours and 15 minutes, but don't count your chickens yet, we haven't even counted the daddy of them all Sunday!!

• Sunday will eat up another 30 minutes getting ready then 2 hours at the kingdom hall and YET ANOTHER 2 hours on service. Plus 30 minutes getting home to do normal stuff and we have an extra 5 hours.

This brings our grand total up to 15 hours and 15 minutes a week! This is 789 hours a year. I have not even counted the 5 days a year at Circuit and District Assemblies which adds 20 hours a year to the total wasted time. An astounding 812 hours per year!! So how could I have spent 812 hours instead?. Let's find out!

Well for starters you could learn to drive. I was a slow learner so it took me 20 lessons at 1 hour per lesson plus some time behind the wheel of my dads car (it didn't help I crashed that car within twenty minutes of passing my test) so let's say 30 hours total. Well you could learn to drive 27 times!!!

Don't fancy learning to drive? OK let's set out sights a bit higher, sky high to be precise it takes at least 45 hours training to get your pilots license, which is awesome! Then you'll need a further 1500 hours to qualify to become a commercial airline pilot, so in just 2 short years you can either be a good Jehovah's Witness publisher on track to be a ministerial servant, a sort of junior Elder, or you'll just get a pat on the back if you are a sister because you have no chance of promotion, or you can be a commercial airline pilot.

You could walk across America! if you keep this up for 10 years you could walk around the Earth! A bit to up in the air for you? Well let's come down to earth with a run, a marathon to be exact, well even of you had one leg and could only hobble it in six miles per hour you could manage 186 marathons a year!

What about your education? Maybe you'd fancy developing your grey matter! What could you achieve with 812 hours every year? Well, my local night school will get you through a GCSE qualification in one year with just 30 hours in the classroom, add to this another 60 studying and doing your homework and you could get not 1 but 9 GCSE's.

Maybe you'd like to go to University instead! Well the University of Leeds has a Chemistry Degree that requires 20 in class per week so you could take that and still have over 200 study and do homework. In 4 years you're either an Elder or a SCIENTIST!!! Albert Einstein or an unpaid lay preacher doing odd jobs to earn a living.

Finally, let's look at a few other options for your 812 hours. You could boil 6090 eggs one at a time!! Get 101 great nights sleep. You could cook 232 Turkeys, one at a time, you could learn 2 different languages! You could become a Java programmer, become an advanced Yoga Teacher, TWICE. You could build 3 ½ sports cars, you could pleasure a woman till her head pops off! Or, if you're like me and can only manage about 15 minutes at best, 812 women 4 times!! You could do SO much more with this precious time but I didn't and I am still paying for that today.

You can see that life as a Jehovah's Witness was very busy indeed! So what were we learning while we were spending hundreds of hours a year at the Kingdom Hall? Well an awful lot about nothing important.

The teachings of Jehovah's Witnesses developed from the thoughts and fancies of a rich white guy called Charles Taze Russel back in the late

1800's. He decided that all other religions were lacking that certain something, his leadership and he set about fixing that problem by starting up a lose association of bible students known as, The International Association Of Bible Students! This group quickly spread around the world and by the end of his life Russel was rich, famous and the beloved patriarch of his own personal cult!

His cult spread due to it's unique and ever changing beliefs. New ideas fell from Russel pen like rain from a cloud and old views became "Old Light" to be replaced by "New Light." If you wanted to be in good standing within your church you had to quickly adopt this new light and just as quickly, forget what you used to believe was literally gospel. This rapid change has carried right through to the present day and shows no sign of slowing down. If I returned to the Witnesses today, well over half the major tenets of my faith would be out of date and unless I quickly abandoned them I would swiftly be kicked out again and labelled an Apostate!

In brief, what we did learn was that we were smack dab in the middle of a spiritual war and we were its front line soldiers. Jesus Christ had come back to earth invisibly at the turn of the century and judged all the religions. He found them all lacking, except for one and despite the fact the one tolerable religion was teaching and practising virtually all the same things as most other Christian faiths he chose them, The International Bible Students. Jesus, who operates as a sort of front man for the ancient Jewish God, Jehovah placed the fate of all life in their hands and gave them the job of preaching to the world until his appointed time to return (again) and put an end to the wicked. If, after hearing their ever changing message, you rejected them then it was as if you had rejected Jehovah and your fate was sealed.

Of course we didn't see it that way. As good and loyal Witnesses we felt that these constant changes, changes that happened so fast that we often had to write notes on new literature to remind us that what was printed a year before was not what we actually believed any more, was OK. It was actually "The Light Getting Brighter". Jehovah's Witnesses were like a ship tacking in a heavy wind, we were told sometimes we go left, other times right, but always moving forward and we needed to be up to date with everything they taught if "Gods War We Would Survive".

You see, when you're raised in a cult you have no basis to decide what is normal and what is batshit crazy and so if you aren't careful batshit crazy can become your idea of normality, which in turn opens a doorway to madness and dishonestly.

As Jehovah's Witnesses we didn't do "Forgiveness" all that well, or "Unconditional Love" or even just "Intelligence". Our job was to go to every meeting, learn what we were told that week and then regurgitate it as often as possible as we went from door to door selling our poorly made magazines and books. In years to come it was revealed that Jehovah was worried about us asking for money for this rubbish so it was made entirely free, for you, not for us, we still "donated" a suggested amount for everything we took. The fact that this prevented the leadership from being accused of tax evasion was purely coincidental.

The constant all consuming nature of this cult was not accidental, it was a deliberate effort to fill up every waking moment in your life so you didn't have a chance to sit back and take stock of what was being taught. It also had the effect of preventing you form improving your life, getting more education or putting in more hours at work. In fact anyone who did feel inclined to do any of those things would quickly get a talking to, accused of "Not Putting Jehovah First In Our Lives", this code word was the first step on a path to trouble. This paths final destination was shunning, isolation and depression.

As a child though, a lot of this was lost on me. I had been put on a road and I was going to walk it to the end. I was fully convinced that I was in the only true religion and I (normally) did my very best to live my life in a the way I was told would be best. As I said earlier I was a true believer. Not for me hiding what I believed to my classmates oh no! I would spend my breaktime as a child trying to "Witness" to other schoolkids, with, mixed results! I would read our magazines, the "Watchtower and Awake", at the back of the Hall as soon as they arrived and I spent a lot of time praying so I could understand "The Deep Things Of God". These "Deep Things" were actually only "Confusing Things" but to the confused anything can be mistaken for deep!

Of course the things I learned had been invented on the hop, by a gang of elderly men with little or no education. Together they sent these teachings out to members as God's inspired word. Failure to understand them meant that you were "Spiritually Immature" and not a candidate for promotion, which should be the goal of any good male Jehovah's Witness. I remember during one summer holidays when I was about 12, I was lying outside on a sunny day with a dozen bound volumes of the Watchtower Magazine, not to mention a half dozen other books and booklets. I had chosen that day to understand the "1914" teaching.

Without boring you unnecessarily the 1914 doctrine is the belief the Jesus Christ began ruling invisibly in heaven since 1914. He also picked the Jehovah's Witnesses as his representatives on Earth, but we've covered that already. This nonsense still needed to be proven and the various leaders throughout history did this by misusing Bible verses and predictions and adding to them the measurements of the Pyramids no less! It's interesting to note that the Pyramid bit was so important to the founder Charles Russell that he had a Pyramid built right next to his grave! When the Pyramid stuff got embarrassing they silently ditched it and tortured even more parts of the Bible in an effort to shoehorn the teaching in.

I tried to figure that crap out for DAYS! I struggled and read, checked the references and ended up being directed and redirected back to where I started. It is safe to say that I never did fully understand 1914 but I have learned enough since leaving to know that all the King James verses in the world couldn't put this Humpty Dumpty back together again!

It may point to some deeper problem with my spirituality or maybe I'm just a dummy but this trend of me wanting to understand our beliefs and just not getting it, was to continue throughout my time as a Jehovah's Witness.

I would continue to struggle with a lot of things. I never understood why you couldn't swear but that getting drunk was a hobby in my hall. I was confused as to why my family really believed it and tried to live like "good witnesses" we were often overlooked and treated badly. As a boy growing up you were taught that the limits of your ambition were to become a full time Pioneer, or cult salesman, and gradually gain promotion from "Publisher" to "Ministerial Servant" and then on to "Elder". Elders were the heads of the congregation and though many were nice you had to watch your step around them in case you warranted "Loving Instruction" from them.

"Loving Instruction" from the Elders usually started out as a conversation from one or more Elders. This could move quickly "Council" and then to "Reproof" all depending on how fast and how low you were prepared to abase yourself. The reasons they came were not really important, I remember one time I was spoken to by an Elder because he had heard me use the word "Flip". Flip is a word roughly equal in severity to "Man" and slightly behind "Heck". It seems that even though it was not swearing, I was actually "substitute swearing" and that couldn't stand! I lay down faster than a whipped puppy and apologised for this terrible crime. If I had argued or defended myself in any way I would have then been in trouble for having a "Spirit of the World".

The crime you committed is not really important you see. Some Elders used any chance they could get to exercise control and as a former member of the Governing Body, Raymond Franz once said "To get anywhere in the Jehovah's Witnesses you have to eat as much humble pie as you can, until it makes you sick" and it was the eating they wanted to see. Free spirits and free thinkers were not welcome, they were quickly winnowed out as a threat to order and by constantly forcing members to beg for forgiveness for imagined sins they could determine who needed the most winnowing!

When I was 11 my sister Karen was 14 and she was not great at crossing the road. She has never been the most coordinated person but on this day she would eclipse all her previous clumsiness by leaps and bounds. As she walked to school she took a short cut over the busy Prince William Road, despite there being a perfectly good tunnel to walk under she walked up the embankment and started across the road anyway. Unfortunately, like a bad Frogger player she only made it halfway. A car travelling about 60 miles per hour hit her and threw her about 200 feet down the road.

Karen was rushed to hospital with... all the injuries. Time prevents me from listing them all but a short recap includes, her legs broken, shattered really, a broken pelvis, ribs and collapsed lungs. The list goes on but you get the picture. Karen was lucky not to die on the road that day and was instead rushed to hospital where she hovered somewhere between "Completely Dead" and "Mostly Dead", she would linger there for the next year or so. This was to be my families entry ticket into the "Deep Things of Jehovah" as we came face to face with their policy on the misuse of blood transfusions.

Using blood is huge no-no for any self respecting Jehovah's Witness. Many thousands of them have made the ultimate sacrifice and died by refusing blood or blood related products. At meetings this rule is constantly reinforced and we had a special yearly meeting where we all got handed little wallet sized cards which had the force of law and commanded any medical professional not to even think about using blood. We signed these with other Witnesses acting as actual witnesses and then they were countersigned by the Elders. We then kept these talisman with us all times, waiting until disaster struck!

Well it struck us hard that day, I'm starting to think my family are unlucky! And as Karen lay near death, the Jehovah's Witnesses sprang into action! In mere hours in rushed the "Hospital Liaison Committee". They arrived to offer support and love, only kidding, they came to make sure Karen died pure and my parents didn't weaken, allowing her to have blood and giving the doctors a chance to actually save her. It was in our darkest hour that an old face reappeared! Yes it was Moses, that Elder who sold my dad a rusted motorbike all those years ago! He was now the head of the Hospital Liaison Committee and how lucky were we!

Time had not turned Moses into a nice guy. Jehovah had failed miserably in his efforts to make a new man out of him because he was still very much the old man my parents had met and been ripped off by. Yet, here he was and his main role was to be a rude and bombastic dick, telling the doctors what to do and then silently hover over my parents, making sure the doctors were not alone with them, during this time Karen was getting worse and worse.

The Jehovah's Witnesses leadership have always loved the rank and file members to be outcasts. In the early days they walked outside churches on Sunday wearing tabards and holding signs saying "Religion Is A Snare And A Racket" in so-called "Information Marches". They discovered that by becoming vilified and reviled they got priceless free publicity and this in turn brought in new members.

They did it again during World War Two by actively denouncing the war and flirting with Adolf Hitler, it seems he had similar feelings about Jews as they did. Once again, they got free news coverage and this was always the point. The leaders were briefly Imprisoned and yet more new members came through the revolving door of the Jehovah's Witnesses. When the war ended and the Governing Body were released, what could they do? Well the first thing they did was to tweak their crazy beliefs so the story of them going into a minimum security prison was actually the fulfilment of Biblical Prophecy! "What now?" they asked each other, then they hit on an idea, blood! It was to be the biggest and most expensive ambush marketing scheme in history!

The Governing Body had suddenly decided that blood was even MORE sacred than God thought it was! No longer could a Jehovah's Witness in good standing even contemplate eating blood or using it medically. This had the effect of making millions of people around the world feel really bad about eating rare steaks and myths began to propagate around the halls about what foods had blood put in them "secretly" in order to make us "Blood Guilty", even today I would shudder if you put a bloody steak in front of me. The programming is deep and long lasting!

It also brought about a medical nightmare that continues today and still takes lives. You see, blood was the symbol of life and the Bible ordered the Israelites to pour it on the ground, therefore anyone who ate or used blood in any way would be breaking God's Law and committing a serious sin. This bizarre and unjustified ruling meant that the symbol of life had become more important than the actual thing and we needed to be prepared to die for that symbol!

Blood was forbidden and so was anything that was made using it. Haemophiliacs with perfectly good outcomes, given modern medical care were left waiting to die, if they wanted to get into paradise. Mothers who started bleeding after birth were faced with trying to explain to doctors that a blood transfusion was not acceptable, a tough thing to do since many of these ladies were quite busy enough with dying.

My sister Karen was a good Witness and would do what was right, my parents were good Witnesses and would not fail Jehovah and in case they did the Hospital Liaison Committee was there to make sure they did what they needed to do.

To you and I the death of a 14 year old girl is a very serious thing but you and I are looking at the wrong way. There are LOTS of 14 year old girls around but advertising is really, really expensive and while the newspaper coverage of a young woman dying because her parents wouldn't allow her to get needed treatment would anger and disgust almost everyone. A few would look and instead see a family dedicated to something they truly believed. They might feel if they were so convinced of it that they'd watch their only girl die, then perhaps they might be on to something!

The policy also served to reinforce the uniqueness of our cult to other members. "This is no game brothers" we'd say. "We are not like those false, once a week Christians. To us it MATTERS, We will die for what we believe". Thus it came to pass that a bunch of uneducated conmen in Brooklyn brought about the deaths of thousands of men, women and children and they have never had to answer for it.

The doctors finally did manage to corner my parents and make them aware of the seriousness of the situation. They were under massive stress and made a deal that whenever Karen was alone the doctors could do what they needed to do but no records were to be kept. Mum and dad only admitted that it happened years later when they had left the cult. They had carried the "guilt" of saving their daughter with them throughout the rest of their time as Jehovah's Witnesses.

Don't Jerk It For Jehovah!

I remember the first time I discovered masturbation. I was about 11 years old and was climbing a tree near my parents house, as I made my way vigorously upwards, by means of a dynamic thrusting motion with my arms and legs wrapped around the trunk, I discovered, what I can only describe as an enormous appreciation for trees! If I had possessed the words, I would have smiled, said "I love you baby" and slip down the trunk to have a little nap beside it, but instead I just chilled out and lit a cigar!

At the start, I didn't even know I was masturbating! I just thought that I really loved trees and this was my reward for putting in the work of climbing so many of them. Quite frankly, with rewards like that, I was willing to put in any spare time I had to perfect the art!

A little later, I discovered that masturbation and trees were not synonymous and you could achieve the same results much more easily and without splinters, so I quickly quit my fledgling "tree sex fetish" and moved indoors.

Imagine my surprise, when I found out that you could masturbate pretty much any time you wanted and it was SO MUCH better than chocolate or Coca Cola! Unfortunately, I was soon to learn that it was also a terrible sin against Jehovah God and would, if left unchecked, make me a "Dysfunctional and Selfish", "Socially Crippled" raging Homosexual!

It was not enough that I had literally found the most fun thing to do with your clothes off, but I was also "Sick" and needed "Cured". Thankfully, if anyone can help young boys with their sexual issues it's middle aged men cult leaders!

I know what you're thinking, "Thank God Neil's warning us about this hidden destroyer of young men and women across the world!. That's right! for without this timely warning, we are in danger of letting kids learn about their bodies in private and with zero chance of catching a disease. When will this madness end!

Thankfully for me, my finely tuned "Christian Conscience" swiftly made me pay attention to all the talks they had at the meetings about it and I finally put two and two together, rand realised that my now, favourite hobby, was actually this so called "Self Abuse" that the Elders had been warning about for so long!

I was very lucky to have had dozens of articles to read which purported to offer advice on how to quit my "Chicken Choking" habit. A brief look back finds over 40 articles about the subject during my formative years, with such stirring advice such as this, found in the Watchtower magazine 1973 but repeated throughout my teenage years at meetings and assemblies.

*"As we have seen, masturbation is indeed **a "hurtful desire." It is also "uncleanness,"** for it is an immoral practice, and this explains why the masturbator generally is ashamed of himself and hides his repugnant act from the sight of others".*

Or this wonderful counsel taken from the book "Your Youth Getting The Best Out Of It" published in 1976 under the heading "Masturbation and Homosexuality".

*"Contrary to what many persons think, **homosexuals are not born that way, but their homosexual behaviour is learned and often a person gets started when very young by playing with another's sexual parts,** and then engaging in homosexual acts."*

Or this from the Young People Ask (1989) p.201 Ch.5 Masturbation- How Serious Is It?

"This young woman's experience reveals what is undoubtedly the greatest reason why the habit can be so hard to break. She continues: "Usually I masturbated to release pressure, tension, or anxiety. That fleeting pleasure was like the drink the alcoholic takes to calm his nerves."

So it's true. If you even think of masturbation, you'll very likely become an unclean homosexual drug addict and I promise you, I'm only scratching the surface of the "Advice" the Jehovah's Witnesses offer impressionable kids on this subject.

Well now that we know the dangers of spanking the monkey, how can we prevent it becoming a problem? Let's turn to the wisdom of Jehovah's Witnesses once again and find out In the same Watchtower magazine of 1973 under the sub title "Prevention and Cure"

"Did you know, for example, that mothers and fathers who stroke the genitals of their fretful babies to keep them quiet are unwittingly encouraging them to become masturbators later on? Boys and girls may start to play with their private parts during puberty and, not receiving any counsel against this, the first thing they know they are "hooked" on the habit. And if some know nothing about such self-abuse before entering high school, the chances are they will learn of it from either fellow students or the teachers themselves."

Mothers! Stop touching your kids! It's your fault (isn't it always?) and you need to know it. Presumably every young boy who is ever spanked by a parent develops a some type of bondage fetish as an adult, so watch out for that too! Don't worry I have even more advice!

"At night-time arrange to share a bedroom with other members of the family. Sleep on the side, not on the back or stomach. These are a few suggestions for arranging the daily routine."

Thank god! All you need to do to prevent a teenage boy from acting on his impure thoughts is to tell him to "Sleep on his side"! Do doctors know about this? What happens if, despite all this outstanding counsel you fall back into sin? Well don't worry because the Watchtower has advice on this too!

*"When they occasionally relapse-usually in a state of semi-conscious sleep-they develop deep feelings of guilt and of being unworthy of Jehovah's mercy. For these reasons it is not only helpful but often advisable to **seek the aid and encouragement of a Christian elder.**"*

So if you are a young man or woman, who is racked with guilt and feels unworthy because of their sexual "Sickness", all you need to do is go seek the advice of one solitary "Christian Elder" in confidence. What could possibly go wrong with this plan?! Yeah.... lots.

So, there I was, I had just discovered Atlantis, climbed Everest, sailed single handled around the world, well it felt a bit like that anyway, and now I had discovered that I was actually ill, needed curing and even worse, I was selfish and was hurting Jehovah because of it, what to do?

I spent a lot of time "Sinning", then feeling really bad about it, then praying to Jehovah and saying sorry, then relapsing and praying again. It is funny and sad that a religion that claims to be the only one actually getting "Light from Jehovah", was incapable of realising that instead of helping to give spiritual guidance to young people they were actually setting them up to have lifelong sexual hang ups!

One Sunday morning, I was sitting in the Kingdom Hall and the speaker began to talk about making "A Sacred Oath to Jehovah". A Sacred Oath, I was told, was much more serious than a simple promise. If you didn't keep a promise, due to illness or other circumstances you hadn't committed any serious sin, but if you made a Sacred Oath to Jehovah and then broke it, well there was no hope for you! You would have committed an unforgivable sin and your chances of surviving Armageddon and making it into a paradise earth full of righteous fellow witnesses were non existent.

So why on Earth would you want to make a Sacred Oath? The reasons, we were told, were manifold. By making this promise we really were upping the ante in our worship of Jehovah and it would also encourage us never to break our promise because we would be scared shitless of the consequences to our eternal life of any failure! All in all, if you really wanted to show your "Spiritual Maturity" you would make an oath to Jehovah and stick to it!

As I've already said, failure to follow through on an oath, was one of what we were told, were unforgivable sins and resulted in a death sentence with no possibility of forgiveness. You could pray from dawn to dusk until you died, but Jehovah wasn't having it and you were a goner! Many's the night, as a young boy, when I would lie in bed worrying if any of my childhood transgressions had added up to "Unforgivable Sin" status. Those were the days my friends!

You could make a Sacred Oath to donate a portion of your wage every month or to spend more time going door to door as a Pioneer, you could even promise to read the whole Bible in a year and then you had to keep your promise! I, like a fool, decided that what I needed to finally put an end to my sin, and risk alienation from God and everlasting destruction if I dared to backslide! So, with trembling hands, I knelt at the side of my bed and promised never, ever to masturbate again. Amazingly that didn't work.

I think I lasted five days before relapsing (still a personal best!) and then on top of my guilt I realized that Jehovah would never forgive me and I was doomed to die at Armageddon which was "Any day now".

There is good news to be had I'm pleased to tell you. Despite well over 3 decades of near constant failure with regard to this particular sin, I have not yet turned gay! Nor have I developed severe mental health problems, become socially crippled or unduly selfish. I developed all those problems for completely different reasons relating to being a Jehovah's Witness! The only downside of my failure is the virtual guarantee, that I have no hope of gaining Gods forgiveness and will die unmourned.

So to all you still serving Jehovah's Witness kids out there, relax, everyone does it and I promise Jehovah's not even looking.

How To Lose Your Sister

It's hard to lose a child, really hard. You can't just leave one at the supermarket! the police will return her. You can't forget to pick her up from school, they phone you to remind you. You can only do it through by a careful combination of throwing them out and making the prospect of returning so terrible that they never want to see you again and that's exactly what we did.

Now, I know what you're thinking, "Wow! Your family, and your sister really made a huge sacrifice for your faith, you guys must have really been treated well after that". Nope, not a bit of it.

My dad still struggled in his work life, eventually getting a temporary job taking emergency calls for the fire brigade and we kept on going to the meetings. Karen gradually recovered and met a boy! I'll get into the massive limitations young Witnesses face when searching for that "Special Someone" but for now let me just say that the young man she chose was less than impressive. Michael was not smart, interesting or ambitious but I still liked him. He grew up in a Jehovah's Witness family in our local Kingdom Hall and we were good friends with his family. His mother Gloria died of Cancer when he was younger, I called her "Auntie Gloria" and still visit her grave sometimes.

Knowing Michael, as I did, I am able to understand him a bit better. Michael was regularly beaten by his father Ronnie. Not the occasional slapped bum that most kids get in their childhoods but full on attacks. I remember one Tuesday evening when we were at their house, we had just finished studying the "Book Study" which should have left us full of the fruits of the spirit. Michael was about 13 and told the guests a joke (something about what happens to poop on an aeroplane) Ronnie was so embarrassed by it and took Michael out into the hallway to "discipline him".

I heard Ronnie punching him again and again but then I heard something new! Michael began punching Ronnie back! He hit him a few times before Ronnie regained the advantage and began dragging him down the hall while Gloria screamed at him to stop hitting him. "It's alright Gloria, there comes a time in a boys life when he thinks he can take his dad!" said Ronnie as he beat that boy. A few minutes later Michael came in crying and issued an apology to all the people who had just listened to his beating and we went home trying to forget that night.

When Michael and Karen began dating a few years later both families (now minus Gloria) were quite happy. I liked Michael a lot, he was older than me and had an awesome gold BMX that I loved! It should have come as no surprise when he began beating Karen fairly regularly. The exact reasons why he beat her are still a bit of a mystery to me but I'm pretty sure they amounted to his way of warming up a girl for sex. His method of getting my sister in the mood was ultimately successful and somehow this became known to the elders in my Kingdom Hall.

Karen and Michael (still both teenagers) were taken before the infamous "Judicial Committee" where three older men questioned them separately about the quantity, quality and position of their relations. Michael, who was used to bowing down to bullying men all his life, quickly admitted all and was disfellowshipped for six months. Karen decided that the whole "Cult Life" thing wasn't for her and refused to express regret for her crimes and was also disfellowshipped. Now that I look back on it, I think a good case could be made for saying that my sister was the victim of some pretty standard physical and sexual abuse that led up to, if not, actual rape then certainly coercive sex by a violent bully but that didn't matter to those wise older men. They met with her and despite her nearly dying for her faith only a few years earlier they disfellowshipped her too.

At first this new wrinkle on our families spiritual journey didn't really make to much difference. Karen had a job by now and simply didn't go to the meetings. When we did go we all ignored Michael who sat silently at the back of the hall like a good boy but Karen stubbornly refused to play the game as our Elders wanted her to play it and it upset them and one of them decided to do something that was to cause our family decades of hurt and pain.

Roland Inman is a to this day (miraculously) a friend of mine. He is smart and interesting. He treated me well as a child and taught me rock climbing, which I now teach my children and most importantly he was humble enough to quit the Jehovah's Witnesses shortly after I did. Sadly, at this point in our story Roland was also a devout Elder, the leader of the three man committee that had disfellowshipped my sister and he was pissed!

Roland came to our home one evening and spoke to my parents telling them that due to Karen's unrepentant ways she was a danger to their other two children and must be removed from our company. Mum and Dad loved us but were thoroughly brainwashed and after listening carefully they did as they were ordered and in turn ordered my sister to leave her family.

This was confusing to young Neil, I had always been closer to Karen than my brother but I too was quite the cult member and even as I helped move her into a rented room in Belfast, I thought that we were obeying Jehovah. Karen had a new boyfriend called Patrick who she met at work and he was the cause of many years of trouble for Karen and in years to come, a restraining order for me!

So we abandoned Karen for the sin of being violently bullied into sex and now came the important work of shunning her! No more the of the gentle shunning when she lived with us, this time it was for real and I took to the job with gusto! I remember one evening when I, totally uncoached, decided to write my big sister a letter telling her that we were done. By this time her relationship with Patrick was getting serious and she had begun attending his Catholic Church. Well that was my limit so I wrote her a letter.

Dear Karen

I am writing you this letter to tell you that I don't want anything more to do with you. You need to come back to Jehovah. You need to repent and say sorry so we can be friends. You KNOW the Catholic church is wrong. You know Armageddon is coming soon and you'll die if you don't come back.

Signed

Neil

I was so proud of that letter and I know that by writing it I received the smile of approval from my mother. Looking back on it I see it for what it was, just a small part of a cult mind control system that ripped away the natural bonds of love and affection from family members and made everything about the cult. My letter (and subsequent full time shunning) did nothing to encourage Karen to come back to the "Truth" but it did help to take away my best friend and my sister for many years but more of that later.

Shunning your family is something ever increasing numbers of Jehovah's Witnesses are having to do. As more and more learn "The Truth About The Truth" and leave, or simply run afoul of the ever increasing rules for members they are cast out and their loved ones are put in the same position as my family was all those years ago. Ironically, the saddest part for me wasn't losing Karen. Sure it was unpleasant and I missed her but I was still a young kid and my brother and I drifted closer together so that filled up a lot of the hole Karen's leaving had left in our family.

The thing that I hated most of all was the new spirit of distrust I felt in the Congregation. The feeling back then among the Witnesses was that if one member of a family was capable of betraying Jehovah then surely their was a serious problem within all its members. This meant that both Steven and I were treated as less trustworthy than others and we were often belittled or ignored in the Hall. While other young men "moved ahead with maturity" we were left behind. Despite the behaviour of other young men our age often being bad for anyone, let alone a Jehovah's Witness, we were always last in line for what we saw as privileges or honours.

Steven and I were once forbidden from having any role within the Kingdom Hall for several months, our crime? We both wore cord jackets that were very cool at the time and this was obviously evidence of our worldly nature! On a different occasion we were marked as bad kids because we had slip on shoes, once again the Jehovah's Witnesses displayed how loving and not at all culty they were!

One summer we arrived to work on the Kingdom Hall during a reconstruction project and were instantly awarded the worst jobs. Despite having worked all summer digging foundations on our own when we arrived one glorious Saturday to complete the job with Witnesses from all over Northern Ireland we were shunted to the back of the line.

Out walked the popular kids with their tool belts and began telling us what they were going to build. They took out their new tools and started to cut clean fresh lumber. They built little cabinets and fences while being bathed in the scent of new wood.

"Steven, Neil, take these old paintbrushes" one of the organisers said.

"What are we doing?" I asked.

"You two will be painting the front fence" he replied.

It turns out he had a very good reason for giving us old paintbrushes. You see we weren't just painting the fence, we were staining it and using the most unpleasant preservative known to man, "Creosote". It was the cheapest and most disgusting thing I have ever used. It was a thin sickly looking brown paint that stank of oil and some chemical that prevented wood from rotting but Creosote had so many others uses! It was also wonderful at making your eyes close shut instantly if you let the fumes anywhere near your face. It also brought your hands and arms up into wonderful blisters if the paint dripped off the brush and onto you, not to mention the semi permanent "Henna" style tattoos it made on your skin!

So you can see that Steven and I were given the plumb roles in our Kingdom Hall and no matter what we did in future or how much effort we put in I always felt very much an outsider right up until my last day at the Hall. This happened again years later when I was about 18 as I arrived one hot summer day (yes we have hot days) to help build the brand new Irish Headquarters of Jehovah's Witnesses outside Dublin. I arrived on site and was given the once over by the Brothers in charge.

"Climb those ladders" they said "When you get up into the attic unwrap those big rolls of glass fibre insulation".

"Oh OK" I said and climbed up the ladder, looking around into the hot dark room. I saw the insulation and got started and quickly discovered that glass fibre is a horrible material and without proper face protection you just as quickly begin coughing glass fibre as it enters and settles in your lungs. I climbed down "Can I have a mask?" I said spluttering, at this point I had paid out for contact lenses and my eyes had now taken on the blood red look of Dracula just before feeding on a tender virgin.

"We've run out" the Overseer told me as he and his friends unwrapped plants to put in the garden. "Pull your T-Shirt up over your mouth like this" he said and then helpfully showed me how to do that. I went back into the attic and sat on a roll of insulation with my T Shirt up to just below my eyes and waited....."Hell no" I said to myself and promptly climbed back down, jumped in my car and drove off as fast as I could never to return. It's nice to know that my brief work at Ireland headquarters paid off for the Witnesses as only a few years later they sold the property for a small fortune and moved all administration back to England.

I did see Karen once or twice despite the shunning. She had gotten married to Patrick (who was also a world class asshole) and had moved some distance away so seeing her was rare. Not to mention the fact, that I made little effort to see her and her husband understandably disliked us! I have to be honest and say that my memories of Karen started to go away and as I got older my life before she left was less and less important in my life.

Armageddon is Coming and You're all Gonna Get It!

I grew up both waiting for and in constant fear of, Armageddon. In case you don't know what that is, let me fill you in.

Armageddon is the "The End of this Wicked System of Things". Yes, soon Jehovah God (in the form of his son Jesus) will kill all the unbelievers on Earth and their kids, never forget the kids, because Jehovah doesn't. He'll probably use Meteorites, lightning and earthquakes, we're not too sure, but rest assured it'll be fucking terrifying. He will then go and find Satan the devil, and lock him up in a giant pit which will usher in one thousand years of peace and happiness. All of this is perfectly reasonable and backed by science, but don't ask me to prove it.

When 1000 years is up Jehovah will, for reasons that seem at best churlish, release Satan back into the community in order to test everyone who is now happy and perfect. He also needs to test all those dead folks he brought back to life, that's right I forgot the bit where he brings back all the dead people who lived good lives or never got to hear about him in the first place. It was this last bit that so pissed of the Japanese

I heard this story every other day for 25 years and it never got old, it never made sense either of course! Now, that I'm thinking about it, I have to take issue with God for releasing Satan from prison. It seems to me, that if anyone in history deserved a life sentence it would be him. I can't imagine even the most liberal parole board thinking that he was ready to be reintegrated into society.

"So Mr Lucifer, what are your plans if we decide to release you today?" officer one asks.

"Well, I think the first thing I'll do is pervert the hearts of several billion humans and start a global rebellion against God" Satan replies.

"Ahhhh, didn't you try that once already? It feels to me kinda like you might not have learned your lesson" officer two jumps in.

"Ohhh no, this is a totally new thing. I promise, that if you release me today, you'll be delighted with the results. There will be practically no rapes, thefts or human sacrifice whatsoever this time" Satan stated matter of factly.

"Are you sure? This is really ringing bells with me. It's like deja vu or something, like I went through all that once before and it sucked" officer one questions.

"Nope, this time will be totally new, no piles of human bodies or tiny baby skulls hung from the walls of my underground kingdom. This time I'm all about keeping things light" Satan proudly says.

"Well I don't know about the rest of the panel, but I'm convinced, I think you're free to go" officer two announces.

As a kid there's nothing like worrying whether you'll die at Armageddon. It's even more fun to worry that you might make it but your mum or dad won't and you'll be an orphan in Paradise! Don't worry about it though, as Jehovah's Witnesses have a solution to that problem.

You see Witnesses have for many years been led to believe, through hints and nods and whispered conversations with Elders, that if you lose a son or a daughter, mum or Dad to the dangers of Armageddon, Jehovah will feel your pain and fix it. He's not gonna show anything decent like mercy, of course not! Instead Jehovah's Witnesses believe he will simply wave his wand and make all their memories of the missing loved ones disappear! That's why Jehovah is so awesome!

That's a big part of life as a Jehovah's Witness. Yes, you have to live with a paralysing fear that the people who taught you how to ride a bike will die in agony any day now and that their dead bodies will be left out to be devoured by birds, like a Zoroastrian wet dream. The fear that you'll be left alone in a strange new world without your parents, but don't worry because Jehovah will make you think they never even existed!

As a kid growing up in "The Truth", we talked about Armageddon constantly. We studied books, booklets, magazine and pamphlets, often into the small hours, filled to the brim with horrific pictures of men in heavy metal t-shirts and slutty looking girls all screaming as buildings fell on top of them or roads opened up and they teetered on the edge.

We would read all this material and then study it and I mean *study* it! Hours were spent discussing and then parroting the things they wanted us to say. Grotesque things were read to little kids like these ones,

*"The majority of people living today will probably be alive when Armageddon breaks out, and there are no resurrection hopes for those that are destroyed then."*Kingdom Ministry 1968 Mar p.4[1]

*"By all the evidences this system of things is hastening to its final confrontation with the God of justice at Armageddon. Parents and children who fail to gain the "mark on their foreheads," that is, an adequate appreciation of God's moral standard, are sure to suffer. Parents will be held accountable for their children, and **children will suffer for the failure of their parents.**"*Watchtower 1968 Feb 1 pp.83-84

"Without question the execution of divine judgement upon apostate Christendom and the rest of Satan's world is imminent. Watchtower1984 Oct 1 p.11

We were then made to learn and recite the most horrible information. All in the hope that we would become convinced that the world was

---

1. http://www.jwfacts.com/images/kingdom-ministry-1968-mar-1975.JPG

once good, had gotten worse and was in desperate need of destruction. Jehovah was waiting in the sidelines to hit us hard in order to bring us to our senses and *we needed it, we wanted it, we craved it,* we were like an abused partner convinced that we deserved the next punch, because we talk to much when God's watching the game.

We learned about the ever increasing rates of war deaths, suicide rates and death by plagues throughout History. We learned about earthquakes, famines and storms but most of all we learned about the Doomsday Clock! The Doomsday Clock was a purely symbolic clock invented by The Bulletin Of Atomic Scientists and used by them since 1947 to publicize the dangers to mankind of global nuclear war and nowadays global warming. We heard about this clock all the time, every time it moved forward a second it was pronounced that the end was near!

Nobody ever told me the clock wasn't actually real, so I spent a good deal of my childhood thinking that a giant clock existed in the basement of NORAD where men in white surgical masks pushed the giant hands around! In 1984, the doomsday clock was moved to three minutes to midnight and panic set in. Talks at the Assemblies were full of doom and gloom, everyone was encouraged to drop everything and use the few remaining days in this wicked old system to preach the good news. You can imagine what this atmosphere was like growing up in and what kind of twisted priorities it gave a family. As we speak, the clock keeps moving forwards and backwards and the truth is, that if Armageddon ever does happen the men meeting to move that imaginary clock will be the last to know.

Post Apocalyptic Tree houses and The Secret Survivalist

I was not an energetic child. I didn't play much sports, unless you count Chess and if you do count Chess, you weren't an energetic child either. Team sports weren't allowed as they might put me in touch with actual normal living children and Jehovah's Witnesses are forbidden from letting their kids have "Bad Associations". Even If I had been allowed to hang around with other kids the odds of making life long friendships were against me as I (like every other JW child) was incapable of behaving in a normal way. Picture this fictional conversation made of things I have definitely said to other kids.

Kid 1 "Do you like football?"

Me "No...er, yes"

Kid 1 "What team do you support?"

Me "What's a team?"

Kid 2 "What games do you like?"

Me "Well, I don't play them much unless you count secretly playing chess with my dad or board games with my family"

Kid 2 "??????"

Kid 3 "Want to come round to my house to play after school?"

Me "Well as one of Jehovah's Witnesses I'm not able to play with you because you look a bit dodgy and you might turn me worldly or gay or possibly both"

Kid 3 "OK then" as he backs slowly away.

Kid 4 "Come here and see this dirty magazine I stole off my dad"

Me "Oh no! But I can show you some magazines that will lead you to eternal life on a paradise Earth"

Kid 4 "Jesus Christ! This kid again, who keeps inviting him to play with us?"

Me "Mum, why don't I have friends?"

So, as I said, kids we weren't allowed to join clubs of any kind and even playing in the street with "Worldly" kids was warned against so I ended up spending a lot of time on my own but I was never truly alone because I had one thing with me constantly, the fear of Armageddon!

To me Armageddon was inevitable and immanent. In only a few short years (possibly weeks) society would turn on me and my family and try to devour us! They would rip babies from the arms of mothers, arrest dads and throw kids like me into group homes where we would be beaten with sticks unless we renounced our faith, it was a stressful time!

Add to this the fact that I was a child growing up smack dab in the middle of the Cold War making a Nuclear War very likely and I hope you'll agree that my decision was the only one possible in the circumstances, I became a "Secret Survivalist".

The Survivalist craze was not a common one in Northern Ireland in the 1980's but I had a guide to lead me through it all, his name was John Rourke and he was THE Survivalist. The Survivalist was a series of pulp fiction action novels by an American author called Jerry Ahern. In them the hero "John Rourke" fought off legions of post apocalyptic biker gangs, Russians, Chinese and even Argentinian Neo Nazi's! He also had one thing that I thought was essential for anyone trying to survive the end of the world, a bunker!

John Rourke had his bunker which he built into the side of the Georgia mountains. It was able to keep him and his loved ones safe for 500 years thanks to cryogenic freezing technology he stole from the Commies! Now, admittedly, I didn't have the ability to build a survival retreat into solid rock but I carried my survival spirit with me into everything I did. I remember back when I was 10 and I saw my mother knitting one evening,

"Mum, could you knit me a jumper?" I said.

"Of course Neil, what colour?" she replied.

"Can you make it reversible, white on the outside and black on the inside?"

"Don't be stupid Neil of course I can't. Why would you even want that?"

I didn't have the guts to tell her that I wanted a reversible jumper so I could be undetectable in winter AND at night time! In my 10 old mind, this jumper might be the very thing that saved me when government agents came to take me away!

If that wasn't enough to make my parents wonder what was going on in my head, I made it even easier for them when I asked my dad to help me build a hut. He was happy to do so and knew just the place to do it, beside our garden and through a semi secret door he cut into our fence. When I asked him if I could hide the hinges and make the wooden hut airtight, he shook his head and walked away. I tried stacking it with tins of beans and some bottled water but we were never rich and my parents would have noticed if I'd taken all mums food.

I quickly gave up on an above ground structure to survive Armageddon and moved into some serious bunker design. Like John Rourke, I too would have a retreat to escape the hordes of angry losers who wanted to kill me, like him It would be hidden and stealthy! Sadly, unlike Mr Rourke, I didn't possess explosives for blowing a tunnel into the mountainside or even a mountainside! What I did have was a small piece of woodland behind my parents garden that led up to a busy two lane road and it was there that I began my bunker!

Sadly, I didn't have much in the way of bunker building expertise or any wood to shore up my excavations but like the WW2 prisoners of old, I carried on digging my tunnel deeper and deeper until I could stand up in it. My plan was to then dig another tunnel sideways then expand it and have a secret hideout only inches under the road! I can't imagine the horror my parents would have felt (not to mention the local council) if they had known that I spent several days undermining a busy road or how close I got to achieving it. Thankfully for everyone, it was not to be.

One day, after a I had started on the side tunnel and made good progress, I finished up as usual by hiding the earth and placing my dads shovel in the hole. I then used the one piece of wood I did have to cover the entrance and put leaves and earth over the top to mask the construction. Later that night, as I was brushing my teeth for bed, I heard the next door kids screaming excitedly "I found a tunnel! I found a tunnel!".

"THE BUNKER HAS BEEN COMPROMISED!" I thought in horror.

Filled with dread, I looked out the window to see two kids walking away with my dads shovel and pickaxe. I quickly ran outside and grabbed them back only to discover my bunker had been destroyed, caved in. My dreams of doomsday living ended by a bunch of nosey neighbours which goes to show, you should never trust worldly kids. It's not hard to imagine the harm that this kind of pressure can have on young kids, let alone their parents, if they were foolish enough to believe the rubbish they were being taught at their local Kingdom Hall but at least that's all in the past right? No, it's even worse now.

Even though my generation were fed lies and false predictions about the end of the world, at least it was just words. Some parents were able to brush off the silliness and keep their kids away from the worst excesses of the cult life but today it's different, today they're still threatening that the end is near and this time it's personal! For the last few years the leadership of the Jehovah's Witnesses has been recommending (read commanding) it's members to actively prepare for the end times. They are to do this by having "Go To Bags", presumably "Bug Out Bags" seemed a little too much like something John Rourke would have had.

These bags (which are actually not a bad idea if you live in a dodgy area) are now the thing to have and Jehovah's Witnesses excitedly discuss what to bring with them. Websites have sprung up to satisfy the demand for backpacks with enough space to carry 3 days of food and water as well as a sizeable supply of Bible literature! Here is the type of thing Witnesses are hearing at their meetings, taken from the Sep 2007 Awake magazine.

ARE YOU EQUIPPED TO FLEE?

The New York City Office of Emergency Management recommends that households plan for evacuation by assembling a "go bag"—a durable, accessible, easy-to-transport bag containing important emergency items. The following may be included:

- *Copies of important documents in a waterproof container*

- *An extra set of car and house keys*

- *Credit or debit cards and cash*

- *Bottled water and non perishable food*

- *Flashlight(s), AM/FM radio, cell phone (if you have one), extra batteries*

- *Medication for at least one week, a list of dosages, prescription slips, and doctors' names and phone numbers. (Be sure to replace medications before their expiration date)*

- *First-aid kit*

- *Sturdy, comfortable shoes and rain-wear*

- *Contact and meeting place information for your household, as well as a regional map*

- *Child-care supplies"*

In itself, having an emergency supply is a great idea, especially, if you live in an area where there is a danger of natural disaster. The damage happens when the people being encouraged to prepare for emergencies are also being told that Satan is about to attack them and throw them into prison, take their kids away and even torture them. Think I'm making this up?, think again. A recent video produced by the Leadership of Jehovah's Witnesses and intended for the rank and file members shows a small group of Witnesses meeting together in a basement while outside the sounds of angry mob are clearly heard.

In this video, the congregation is led in worship by a chinless Jim Jones who commends them on keeping the faith. Suddenly, we can hear the voices of gruff men shouting as they search the house, "Where are they" says one.

"Check the basement" replies another.

I am terrified! God alone knows how the children (yes they subjected child actors to this abuse) feel about what's going on! They stand up and hide in a corner as Jim Jones and the rest of the men folk stand in front to protect the women and children, this might be the first time

Jehovah's Witnesses have actually protected women and children. The door rattles as they try the lock it and then in bursts a group of police or soldiers wearing, what can only be described as thrift store uniforms.

The Witnesses look at them sternly, as the soldiers walk closer to reveal riot shields and what look like welders masks and we are left with a final view of the Witness leader looking full of firm conviction, as these bully boys come ever closer. Where's your go bags now guys?

I find it impossible to imagine that the leaders of the Jehovah's Witnesses aren't aware of the psychological harm these videos do to their members. When you combine them, with the admonition to constantly prepare for the end this only reinforces the false belief that Jehovah's Witnesses are a persecuted minority. The fact that, for decades, the Jehovah's Witnesses leadership has orchestrated events in many countries so their own members are imprisoned, raped and tortured, will not be far from the minds of any Witness who sees this video and they and their children will be terrified for the future and even more bound up in cult life.

Here is link to that terrible video if you want to laugh and cry at the same time.

https://www.youtube.com/watch?v=wackkicmf4k

I have since learned, that I was not alone in worrying about and planning for Armageddon. Many other ex Jehovah's Witnesses have told me that the threat of immanent persecution kept them up at night too and they also made plans to escape with their friends and family. As I said at the start of this book I still remember as a very young boy, the feeling of holding my fathers hand and asking him what he'd do when the authorities came to take us away from him. Jehovah's Witnesses are taught to constantly look out for signs that the end is upon us and like them I still do. It's a hard habit to break it seems.

Often, I find myself reading the news and thinking the worst about any given situation. My daydreams are often about my building ideal bunker and I watch Doomsday Preppers with envy. I get emails regularly from ex cult members who are petrified that every sad news story is just a prelude to Apocalypse and it has become my job to tell them to relax and take one day at a time.

Once in the distant past a poor Roman citizen watched in horror as the Gauls stormed her city. A Christian ran in terror from the forces of Attilla The Hun and even my own grandmother slept in hedgerows to escape German bombers while pregnant with my mother during World War Two. Those people carried on, so did life and so, hopefully will we.

Schooldays As A True Believer

Kids growing up as Jehovah's Witnesses will have many things in common, this helps us all to have a sort of collective experience that bonds us together even today. I feel most at home with Ex Witnesses. I still enjoy the rare occasions that an ACTUAL Jehovah's Witness talks to me but that doesn't happen often.

By far the most memorable part of my Witness life was as a child in school and one of the things I remember most during my school years was the near constant bullying. The first school I went to when I returned from Canada was Killowen Primary School in Lisburn and as far as I know my brother and I were the first Jehovah's Witnesses they had ever met, that was going to be a problem.

I know that whatever your colour, faith or personality type most children will face bullying at one time or another. It's also very hard to judge whether or not a child is being bullied because kids are cruel and love to mock things that are different, or that the poor bullied kid can be somewhat responsible as well. What I DO know is that a child who grows up as a Jehovah's Witness is carrying a big backpack full of crazy on their shoulders and throughout their academic lives those poor kids are encouraged, by both parents and Elders alike to empty all that crap out on their desk and show it to everybody!

As a devout little kid I was eager to participate in my own destruction in school. I honestly listened throughout the meetings. I read the magazines and all of these were warning of the upcoming day of Gods judgement against mankind, who wouldn't want to warn their classmates and neighbours if their sudden destruction was so near at hand? So armed with Jehovah's Witness literature I bought with my own pocket money I would go to school to "Witness" to anyone who would listen, they did not listen, what they DID do was bully.

Bullying from students or bullying from teachers, it didn't matter and it was something I had to deal with throughout my life in school. I grew up in a time and in a country where religion mattered very much, even today it matters. So you can imagine the reaction of a bunch of middle aged Christian ladies to an 8 year old boy who walks into class with a funny accent and asks that his religious liberties be respected while repeatedly demanding that they adjust decades of school policy to fit his needs?

My first teacher of note was called Mrs Campbell, she was a tremendously mean lady who looked the other way as I was ridiculed and mocked. On one occasion when I was 8 years old, I had sneaked away to avoid the other children and accidentally returned late from lunch. As the class lined up outside waiting for me to arrive, she marched up to me and smashed her coffee cup across my head. This was back in the days when teachers didn't get into trouble for much of anything, it broke across my head spectacularly but it was not the worst of what was to come.

The next year I moved to a new teacher Mrs Sloan. She was a born again Christian, which is a term I always had with a suspicion of because of her and she took it as a great insult that she was forced to tolerate me in her class.

Mrs Sloan decided it would be fun to get me to stand in front of the class and then get them to ask me what I was getting for my birthday or Christmas. If I didn't want to do that then she would hit me or throw things at me. I remember another boy in class whose mother was studying with the Witnesses, she tried to do the same to him and when he refused she backhanded him across the classroom, her diamond ring leaving a deep cut in his face.

My parents were good people however, and knew that school should not be like that. By time I had spent about two years in Kindergarten, when we still lived in Canada and the school there had had no issue with our beliefs. I remember refusing to stand for the national anthem every morning with no problems at all, even years later I can still sing every word to "Oh Canada" despite having not lived there for over 35 years! Perhaps it was the huge influx of children from around the world that meant those teachers were ahead of their time but whatever the reason I still look back to my short time at Brookmede Elementary School In Mississauga with happiness and I would like to thank them for taking the time to try to show love and understanding to a little child trapped in a cult.

Mum and dad marched to school to complain about Mrs Sloan, "No one has ever complained before" the Headmaster told them. "You're too sensitive" he said. Mum and dad left only to return days later after the latest episode of cruelty "It didn't happen" the Headmaster said. "Why is it only you who complains" he asked. Mum and dad would later find out that multiple parents had complained about this evil woman and not just the children of Jehovah's Witnesses, it seemed she took pleasure in torturing children and the school had in place a cunning plan to avoid blame. Deny it for a few more years and let the bitch retire. It was then that mum and dad did something I was will always be grateful grateful for, they took me out of school and taught me themselves. Years later, when I was about 16 I sneaked into the school and scratched "Sloan is a Bitch" on her classroom door, this still cheers me up!

One bright spark in those dark days was when I was chosen to take part in the school play. This was a religious play and would take place in a special assembly where the Headmaster would say a prayer. This was of course as big no-no for me but I really wanted to do it and after begging my mum and dad they relented and I stood with great pride in my fake Israelite robes and shouted out "The Governor from the Northern Embassy my lord" I have no idea to this day what the play was about but I was chosen for this plumb role by virtue of how loud I could shout my line and I can still shout pretty loud, ask my kids! Of course, I had to hide my delight in being in this play from anyone outside the family as my parents would have gotten in trouble from the Elders for allowing this terrible act of false worship.

I admit that I had painted a target on my back in those days, well I was encouraged to paint it on my back while my parents and the Elders held my hand to make the "Kick Me" sign even bigger and neater so more people could see it! I still find it hard to believe how mean people can be given a little encouragement. As the years went on I would get called "You Jew Bastard" by other kids, presumably Jehovah's Witnesses were a rarity and so any religious insult was acceptable! I took great efforts to explain that I was NOT a Jew (though it now turns out I am at least 40 percent Jewish) "I am a Jehovah's Witness" I would say in exasperation, but since this was Northern Ireland in the middle of our Sectarian Civil War, I was met with the question "Yeah, but are you a Protestant Jehovah's Witness or a Catholic Jehovah's Witness".

When I was 9 or 10, I got into the habit of hiding a small pair of roller skates in my school bag every day. I would wait until lunch and, in an effort to avoid being bullied, would run out of school and put my skates on. Then I would hobble across a grassy verge and leap into the busy traffic on the main road that ran to my parents house. I did this many times and probably terrified more drivers than I can count but doing so allowed me to go home and eat lunch with my mum and not with the kids who took delight in making my life hell. I told my mother about this but she claims I made it up as she would never have let her youngest child roller skate down a busy main road but she's wrong, I remember it and It was awesome!

It was with great joy that mum and dad took me out of school and as was Witness custom where possible, home schooled me. Back in those days this was unheard of! Parents were to do as they were told and children were to sit down and shut up so home schooling was really a big "Screw You" to both the school, the teacher and the Education Authority and even though my mum was now my teacher, it was miles better than staying with Mrs Sloan.

When I turned 12, I moved to Laurelhill High School and entered the big time, I was older now and at the height of my religious fervour. So for sure, I carried on as before doing the usual nonsense, preaching to my classmates and exposing myself to bullying by refusing to take part in anything that even sniffed of religiosity, but nothing I did made me happy or most importantly, made me a better person.

My home room teacher was Mr Ray. He was a nice chap with a tendency towards lecturing us on Socialist Politics when he should have been lecturing us in William Golding and Shakespeare. I think I owe him a debt as he prevented the worst excesses of my cult inspired stupidity. I once asked Mr Ray if I could give a talk to everyone in my class about my beliefs, I would even do it at Assembly if he could arrange it! I had already bought literature to hand out and was ready for action, thankfully he said no.

At first I thought I was being "Persecuted", I thought that my chance to "Witness" to my school had been cruelly stolen away from me and it bothered me, so I asked him again and when he said no I bravely asked him why. "Because this is a school not a church Neil. If I allow you to do a talk about what you believe what's to stop everyone doing a talk and who's correct?" This flawless logic still left me disappointed as of course my truth was the only real "Truth" so this seemed pretty unfair.

Can you imagine the sheer quantity and quality of bullying that I would have gotten if I had done that talk? I can and it still scares me that I came so close to disaster. If Mr Ray had been any less of a decent and thoughtful a man I would have gained the attention of every bully around and deserved every minute of it.

I'd love to tell you that I went through school in a manly, Christian style, that I stood tall for my beliefs like Shadrack, Mesheck and Abed-nigo when they were ordered to bow down to the image of the king of Babylon but I wasn't taught to do that. Instead, I was taught to make things worse for myself, complain, claim persecution and most importantly to kick down. Years of Jehovah's Witnesses "Education" had trained me to tell on anyone for anything and then when they got in trouble feel glad it wasn't me. So, I'm ashamed to admit it, I picked on other, weaker kids when they were being bullied, it kept the bullies away from me for a while. I wasn't a teachers pet because I put far too little effort into school for them to appreciate me and I was as likely to tell them about Jehovah as was to discuss a maths problem!

The only time my religious idiocy helped me was when a slightly weaker kid than I made the mistake of bullying me. David was a follower of other bigger kids. He would wait until they picked a victim and jump into attacking them with gusto. I was walking home after school as he rode past me on an old rusty bike, his new one having been stolen the day before.

Now, David and I never got along but I couldn't do much about it as he was protected by tougher boys, "Nice bike David" I said sarcastically. You might say I deserved it but David answered this insult by aiming a glob of spit directly into my mouth and riding on. The adult in me has to admit that this is an accomplishment worthy of applause but it's still a little raw for me to do that so you can go ahead clap, I'll wait.....

As I've said David and I had a history going back five long years. Much of it involving him sneering, spitting, punching and generally being an asshole while I prayed him and his mates would leave me alone but this Olympian spit was the limit. All weekend I thought about this and prepared my revenge. Monday came and I went into school and waited patiently through the morning register, we then filed out of the classroom to head to our first lessons of the day, not me though. I shadowed David like a particularly close shadow, as usual he was one of the last out of the room. The heavy door swung closed and we were both in the dark hall. I ran towards him, grabbed the back of his head and pushed him face first into the wall as hard as I could. I then repeatedly rammed his head into the bricks screaming "Stop being mean to me!". David crumbled onto the floor crying and bleeding and I walked off to Art class with a smile on my face and joy in my heart. This lasted at least ten minutes until the Deputy Headmaster came to find me and took me away.

"Why did you smash David's face into the wall Neil" he asked.

"I didn't, he fell" I said.

David was having trouble forming words at this point and just stood their angrily shaking his bloodied head back and forth. "Well Neil, I know you're an honest boy and wouldn't lie to me and even if something did happen between you both of you must be at fault. So I'm going to leave this now". The Deputy Headmaster made us shake hands and nothing more was said. I like to think that the five years of hell I had put myself through had paved the way to my getting a pass that day. Though I still got bullied after that David was never interested in taking part again.

I look back on it now and feel a lot of hurt, though not a much hurt as David! I feel cheated out of the chance for a decent, quality education. Cheated out of the opportunity to make friends, join clubs or be a normal child but most of all I feel cheated that I never had a chance to develop as an ordinary human being. I can't blame school for all this though, they offered me the same chances as any other child going through the system. The real culprits responsible for making my time in school miserable and for taking away the chances to go further were closer to home, The Witnesses, my parents and myself.

The Jehovah's Witnesses teach children that school is of only secondary importance at best. They put all their emphasis on making children mini-preachers and then send them out into the world, this often leads to them being horrifically bullied but don't worry they have the answer for that, tell them it's Satan's fault. That's right, whenever a Witness child is bullied for their beliefs (which aren't really theirs) it's the Devils fault and not the men and women who encouraged them to stick out like sore thumbs from their classmates. Whenever they return home miserable and isolated they are told "See, that's what Worldly people are like", this explanation then pushes them to draw even closer to the very group that's destroying their childhood.

I did as little as possible during my five years of Secondary School. What's the point? as Armageddon was coming "Any day now" as they told us at every meeting. So I coasted where possible and ignored those lessons I felt useless or blasphemous. One day in biology class we began to study the theory of evolution and I decided I had no need to listen to the teacher. "I know all about this" I thought."I have studied the Creation book three times!" The Creation book, or to give its full title "Life How Did It Get Here By Evolution Or By Creation" was a large blue book that we studied many times to learn why evolution was wrong, why it's proponents were idiots and why Jehovah was really the creator of everything. Now I honestly don't mind what you personally think about this issue, I have no strong opinion, though despite reading dozens of books on the subject though if you put a gun to my head I'd have to pick the side with the scientists on it over the side with the Jehovah's Witnesses!

To get a small idea what my sole authority on the theory of evolution was like let me quote just a few reviews of this old book.

*"This book grossly misrepresents the Theory of Evolution. It defines the the-
ory as something that it is not, and then proceeds to argue against that
thing. This is an informal fallacy known as a Strawman.*

*It also commits a fallacy known as the Argument from Ignorance. The way
the book commits this fallacy is by trying to prove creationism by poking
holes in evolution. If the Theory of Evolution was proven false tomorrow,
it would not add a single ounce of evidence to the creation hypothesis. Instead of providing evidence for its position, it says, Look at how evolution
is wrong. If evolution is wrong, it must have been God.*

*Not only that, but it has many factual errors and misapplications of sci-
ence"*

Or this gem -

*"Please, do not purchase this book. I urge you to be honest with yourself
and your search for truth. This book is so inaccurate, that a wiki entry was
created to point out the over 130 inaccurate entries in this book".*

Finally, this review -

*"Totally dishonest presentation, designed for the scientifically uneducated
and rhetorically gullible".*

Of the many, many misleading statements and misrepresentations
found in this book, the quotations of Sir Richard Dawkins are among
the most flagrant. Happily, he calls them out on this in one of his
books, *The God Delusion*. A video exists of Professor Dawkins and his
wife reading that section of the book; just You Tube *"Richard Dawkins
Debunks Watchtower".*

As you can see, I was well prepared to ignore my teacher as she ex-
plained Evolutionary Theory to the class, so I lay my head down and
used the time wisely to get some sleep. Miraculously I did not fail my

Biology exams, although my potential career as a Doctor was cut short before it even began, which was handy as I had only one firm plan in my life, to become a full time Pioneer Preacher for the Jehovah's Witnesses!

On the day I left school, early of course because "Why not?" a seagull shit on my head as it flew over me. Due to a pretty poor education I think it's safe to say that life has carried on where that seagull left off.

Interludes Where I Am The Hero

I grew up in what is basically a pacifist cults (so long as you don't count beating your kids, which was highly encouraged!) my options for doing traditionally manly things were extremely limited, team sports, martial arts, self defence, even non cult books were strongly discouraged. When other kids were in Boy Scouts learning to camp, I was learning how to present the magazines more effectively door to door. When those same kids were watching action movies, we were being encouraged to throw out our TV's. When the Army Cadets were taking my classmates out for a drive in a tank, I was playing with Star Wars figures minus the guns, because my parents had thrown them all away!

We would read and then study exciting (for us at least) stories of intrepid missionaries who travelled to distant lands and swan through crocodile infested swamps with the latest Watchtower magazine, rolled up and clenched in their teeth. God alone knows where they stored the books! We were in awe as these modern day Apostles held secret meetings in countries where we were banned and went door to door as the police hunted them down like, and sometimes with, dogs. We cried as our Brothers were arrested and prayed for them when we learned about the long prison sentences they got for serving Jehovah.

For the young Neil, these stories left open the possibility that I might see the world and maybe have an adventure and *still* please Jehovah. That I could serve something greater than myself and dammit, BE A HERO. What young person doesn't dream of leaving their home town one day, doing great things and returning with amazing stories?

One day, I wanted the magazines to tell the story of me. How Neil went around the world saving people for Jehovah while risking his life. How at every turn, I left the wicked servants of Satan angry and gasping as I blanketed their police states with leaflets and Bibles. Well, I was only

12 and this was what passed for day dreaming, but sadly it was never to be.

The problem was not a ridiculously high opinion of my own abilities, or even the fact that I could never swim through a malarial swamp without goggles and nose clips, never mind outrun the crocodiles. It was, because I lived in an area "Where the need is greater" so I had zero opportunity to do anything exciting outside the tiny country I lived in. In fact, the mere thought that you might want to leave your "territory" and live abroad was considered a selfish and potentially rebellious thing to do!

Not for me, adventure and foreign travel, I had to set my sights on Ireland and be satisfied. The percentage of Witnesses to Worldly people was much too low and they needed us right here! The closest I would ever get to a tan was going to be getting burned from sitting to close to a peat fire in Co Cork. The closest I was ever to get to a tropical forest was buying a second hand mahogany wardrobe from Goodwill. The closest I'd ever get to seeing the West Indies was touching the cork board at the back of the Hall.

Instead of excitement and adventure, I'd get chilblains and boredom and despite what you might think, Ireland in the winter is no place to write adventures stories about. Back in 1968, Chinese food was considered a radical risk to your health, McDonald's was a distant rumour and the nearest pizzeria was over a 100 miles from my house! My town of tens of thousands had only 2 black people and everyone knew their names! In short, it was dull.

My lack of excitement was further compounded because my Kingdom Hall was not a very friendly place. It was riven with different cliques, as are all Kingdom Halls and any opportunities for excitement, such as they were, were limited to those who knew and were friends with, the right people. One slightly fun thing we could do was to join the "Quick

build Team". Back when I was younger the Jehovah's Witnesses were on
a bit of a role. They were in an expansion phase and needed lots of new
Kingdom Halls. The Witness leadership like uniformity in all they do
so they had a few approved designs and then, after the local Brothers
dug and laid the foundations. They held a "Quick build" on a special
weekend.

Quick builds served two functions. First, they allowed a Hall to be
built extremely quickly and cheaply using hundreds of men and women
who would come from miles around to build it for free. They would
stay in tents and living rooms and work long into the night, all with the
goal of completing the building in just 48 hours! Secondly, the whole
thing was a show for the locals, a religious advertisement and a show
of strength that might encourage outsiders to ask who these dedicated and impressive people were and maybe even give them a hearing the
next time they called at their door. Impressed newspapers often ran two
page articles about the spectacle and this was used to tell the world that
we were here and we meant business!

Quick builds seemed to me like a wonderful adventure and lots of
young kids my age were taking part. They were learning new skills, travelling the length and breadth of Ireland and the UK and when they returned, they shared some of the stories I wanted to have. So, I decided
one day to ask our local quick build leader "Ralph" if I could join his
team.

Ralph held the awe inspiring and very important role in the quick build
hierarchy of "Plaster Board Leader". This meant that he was responsible
for putting up drywall after actual people with real skills had built the
walls and installed the electrics. His team would then sweep in, stick in
some insulation and then nail on lots and lots of drywall. For this key
role, both Ralph and his "Team" needed a veritable arsenal of tools and
of course belts to hang them on. I am convinced that there is some truth

to the old saying about some men needing to buy big expensive toys to compensate for other inadequacies, because Ralph loved to show off his toys given half a chance!

I remember Ralph very well and even though he still does his best to shun me, I always say hello as we pass on the street. Ralph was larger than life, a giant of a man. He was an Elder in our Hall and he took command of the room wherever he went. He had funny stories and made me think that he was what a man should be, what I should be. Sad to say, he was not and it took me a long time to realize that he was actually a terrible role model.

His drinking was legendary and would eventually result in his humiliation and loss of all responsibility in our Hall but at that time, I really looked up to him and even though I tried to impress him and make him like me, I knew that he didn't and that he had some younger kids he was more interested in and enjoyed spending time with. They had gone to his old school and played in the school sports teams which should have disqualified them from anything that even smelled of fun but somehow it did not. So, I was nervous about approaching Ralph but I really wanted to be a part of the adventure that was quick builds.

I knew, that to get on the team, I needed to spend more time on the door to door work in order to be in "Good standing in the congregation" so I did just that. I spent several months making sure I was doing enough, I went out on Field Service on Friday nights and Sunday afternoons. I even went out on the occasional Saturday! So I knew that I had the basics covered when I approached Ralph. I would be young to be on the team but had some reason to be confident that I would be allowed to join, my family were pretty good witnesses. I was doing everything I needed to do and Ralph already had younger people on the team so why not me?

I walked up to Ralph after the Meeting one Thursday "Excuse me can
I talk to you" I asked. Ralph led me to the back of the hall and waited
for me to speak, "I want to get the application to join the Quick Build
team" I said. He stood there for a moment looking down at me and
then asked what was the most stupid and cruel question, "I'm not sure
Neil, what experience do you have?".

What experience did I have? What experience did I have?! He had
known me since I came back from Canada at the age of 7. He had seen
me 3 times a week AT LEAST, every year since then and I was only 12.
When did he think I was out getting experience in the building trade?
Did he think that local builders were recruiting child labour or that my
tree house was split level and fully plumbed?.

Of course, I had no experience and Ralph knew that. He also knew
that I was a dedicated true believer and he had no interest in having me
anywhere near him when he went away to various quick builds. I later
learned it was because he had turned the quick builds into marathon
drinking binges with his friends, the younger kids on the team knew it
and weren't likely to tell on him. I, on the other hand would have run
off to my parents the minute I saw any wrongdoing so Ralph was probably smart to palm me off that day but I saw it as a huge rejection and it
was the first time that I realised that nothing I could do would ever do
good enough to please the Elders.

While the other boys on the quick build team would carry on half-ass-
ing their spiritual lives, one would also get made a Ministerial Servant
in the Hall. I was no good. While Ralph continued his drywalling and
binge drinking weekends, I began to allow my doubts in the truth to
grow and was forced to accept that perhaps I couldn't have a happy ful-
filling life and still be a Jehovah's Witness.

Years later I would learn that Ralph (who was responsible for our Local
Kingdom Hall accounts around the time our Congregation mysteri-

ously lost tens of thousands of pounds) had been the victim of an out of control barbecue which had spread to where he kept all our financial records.

This of course was completely accidental and not at all suspicious.....

The Life Of A Pioneer, Try Six Months

So, as I have already told you, school was no picnic for a Jehovah's Witness well certainly not my one! It was nearly impossible to make or keep friends. Interactions with students and teachers was uncomfortable at best and I rarely felt good in my own skin. Gaining an education was not encouraged and since so much of what I did learn directly contradicted what I believed to be true, I honestly thought I was taking my school bag into Satan's lair every day!

I cringe when I think back to that old Biology class! As other students were learning the theory of Evolution (It's more than just a theory kids!) I was scoffing in the back because I knew the truth! And the truth was gonna get me to paradise, not this monkey business.... see what I did there?

As my compulsory education was coming to an end I began to consider the several options open to me! I could carry on at school eventually moving on to higher education, back then this would have cost me LITERALLY nothing or I could go to a trade school while at the same time "Serving my time" with a private company. After working for 4 years I would end up as a plumber, a carpenter or an electrician ALSO FOR FREE! Or I could pack it all in and start working part time in a dead end job while at the same time working for free begging money for poorly made religious books and pamphlets which offered door to door, can you guess which one I picked?

I feel that right now I want to make it clear that a lot of my life decisions were not massively influenced by my parents. Instead years and years of attending meetings and assemblies had so warped my mind that I actually thought that this was the best thing to do with "The short time left". "Why should I go back to school after the hell I have just been through?" I thought. "No way! I'm getting out as fast as I can, I need to be free from this as soon as possible".

I didn't understand that school is often a miserable experience for MOST kids. Instead of being told that fact, I was taught to believe that this was how "Worldly" people behaved and so my desire was to stay as far away from them for as long as I possibly could.

I did seriously consider going to trade school, the fact that Jesus got away with it too and became a carpenter before becoming the Son of God, was usually a good enough excuse for a young man to do the same. Even then, I decided against it as this would mean more years in school hanging around the same people who had already spent years mocking and abusing me. Even if I didn't have to be near them, I was still very much aware that the end of this system was coming very, very soon!

The United Nations "Year Of World Peace" had been celebrated in 1986 and here was I in 1991! "It couldn't be much longer" I told myself hopefully. This was further impressed on my mind when an Elder, in my hall, Jim Ireland told me "There is NO WAY you'll see 25 years old in this wicked old system!". So what was a young man to do? You guessed it! Just like Tracy Chapman did in the song "Fast Car", I quit school to look after my elderly alcoholic father, except my father was a cult and boy did he need looking after!

Becoming a "Full time Pioneer" for the Jehovah's Witnesses is a very important job, that requires zero qualifications. You don't need any exams or even need to be able to read very well. All you need is to be prepared to walk miles and miles every week with a book bag and a smile, and the smile is optional most of the time. Back in my day there were 3 types of Pioneer in a Kingdom Hall:- the Auxiliary, the Regular and the Special. At any one time in Ireland, there may also be "Missionaries" who were sent directly from the Jehovah's Witness headquarters at Brooklyn New York, but I'll go into more detail about them a bit later.

Note to young readers: If you think your job is important and it took virtually no effort to get it, it is most likely not that fancy! This includes virtually all door to door sales positions, outbound call centre jobs and anything that popped up online when you were surfing for porn!

I remember walking up to my mum in the kitchen after school one day and asking her what she would think if I became a Pioneer. "That's fine with us Neil" she said "we'd be very proud of you" little did she know that I would actually follow through on my rash idea!

I wish now she had looked at me and instead said "Are you crazy child? you are not even grown up and there is no way on Earth, your father and I will let you waste your life traipsing around from door to door selling books! You are either getting a decent job or going back to school" but mum and dad thought the end was near too and therefore this was a good idea. So, off I went to put in my application for the full time ministry.

I was worried about immediately becoming a regular Pioneer, as the time requirement was pretty daunting. The 3 different levels of service each required a larger amount of time spent on the door to door ministry. First 60 hours per month, then 90 and then over 100. So, I decided to start off with "just" the 60 hours and in the month of October 1991, I started what was bound to be a productive life in Jehovah's service working as an "Auxiliary Pioneer".

I first set out to get the "Pioneer Uniform". In my hall, that meant several warm jumpers, a book bag and a lined trench coat. An especially wise Pioneer would also have some charcoal hand warmers and a woolly hat. You can still spot the pioneers in Ireland by how warmly wrapped up they are for a day in the cold!

Becoming a Pioneer is a mixed bag, you have just entered into the holy of holies. You are a FULL TIME MINISTER OF JEHOVAH! You are also flat broke and to those "worldly" peers in your congregation a cautionary tale about what NOT to do with your life. While they are setting out on bright futures and having new experiences you are doing, exactly what you have always done! walking slowly from door to door giving away magazines to unenthusiastic homeowners and hoping that they'll pay a few pennies to "cover the cost of printing".

It seems sad when I think back on it, but those pennies actually made a difference to me and I was super excited to get them! That was, until the Governing Body changed how we sold the literature. You see instead of selling them, we gave them away, but first WE had to pay for them! any donations were then also to be handed into the local congregation. This meant that they got paid twice for the same old crap and I lost out on money that could be better spent buying chocolate!

I was pretty serious about doing things right as a Pioneer. I got up early and walked to the "Service Meeting" where I met up with other chilly preachers. There we talked about our plans for our day in "Field Service". We'd read a few Bible verses then drive off, or in my case walk off, to our assigned territory to get to work.

If you think this sounds like a sales job, you are absolutely right. The whole system of placing literature and ultimately gaining converts has been set up like a sales pitch for decades. We even had a book specifically designed to make us learn the ABCs of selling, (Always Be Closing). This book was called "Reasoning From The Scriptures". It answered every possible question that might be thrown at us and allowed us to turn every "no" into a "maybe", at least that was the plan, usually we got told to clear off and then we started all over again at the next door.

The way Jehovah's Witnesses sell religion is in no way different than the way a guy sells vacuums or knives door to door and if you know a lot of Jehovah's Witnesses you'll probably discover that many are currently involved in sales jobs. Even after we leave the cult, we find selling is bred into us as kids and we tend to do very well at it. Speaking for myself, sales has never been far removed form how I earn a living and I can't see that changing any time soon.

Getting back to my Pioneering, I tried to be a good pioneer. I kept excellent records

Mr Smith says "Never come back here again!"

Mrs Jones's husband has died - get "When Someone You Love Dies" brochure

Buy Long Johns-my balls are freezing!

I went out often with the various weekly groups. This was encouraged partly as a "Strength In Numbers" kind of thing, but also to make sure you weren't lying in bed and faking your hours! It was many years later that I learned of the sneaky tricks Pioneers use to make those hours come a little more easily!

The first trick to do is to knock on a door near your own home then walk slowly, often several miles to meet up with others. The walking time then counts! then you finish up a morning by repeating step 1 and instead of all that walking time being wasted and uncounted-it is simply just wasted!.

You can also get involved in more impressive tricks to "Get Your Hours". Some I never tried include "Phone Banks". This is where a groups of Pioneers get together and phone random people to "Share the Truth". This is a great way to spend a cold day inside and means you only have to make a call every hour or so and every second can be counted!.

You can also write letters! Just pick some unlucky sap from the phone book and send them a letter about how awesome Jehovah is! if you want to clock up some serious hours just photocopy the letter and send it to multiple people, you can then count all those letters as if you wrote them by hand!! This one might get you in trouble if you mention the copier but trust me, plenty of people have tried and gotten away with this one!

I knew several Witnesses who cruised the local obituaries and then sent the bereaved letters to tell them that they might see their lost family member in Paradise, if only they start a study with Jehovah's Witnesses. If any of this sounds strange or creepy, it's because it really is pretty gross.

One trick every Witness knows, regardless of their position, is the "The Pioneer Walk". This method of time wasting is so famous, it is known around the world and practised by all at one time or another. To get an idea of "The Pioneer Walk", imagine you are walking along in a funeral procession- peaceful, serious, dignified, purposeful, SLOWLY. Slowly is the key to "The Pioneer Walk" as it allows your time spent out on service to be taken up with as little talking to your neighbours as possible. If you are getting strange looks from other more dedicated Witnesses, simply pull out a notebook and start writing about the last call, instant cover!

Closely related to "The Pioneer Walk" is "The Soft Knock", this can also become "The Soft Ring" if the householder has a doorbell. To pull this off you have to walk up to the door taking manful strides, even if you're a woman, and bring your knuckles rushing towards the door as if you have no other objective than to get the owners attention. Then you stop the instant before you hit the door and tap ever so lightly, as if the door was a butterfly and you were stroking its head. You can then wait for AGES while no one answers, if someone does open the door, despite your best efforts, you just pretend you knocked anyway or the bell is broken. This last excuse has led to more than one awkward moment in my life as the homeowner then rings their own bell and stares at me. These methods are all fully endorsed by Jesus........shut up!

When you consider that I didn't know about these tricks until long after I had given up Pioneering and had actually walked around my home town for 60 hours a month, you might understand why I quickly discovered that I hated preaching to others and I hung up my boots after a mere 6 months. Unfortunately, my belief that I was doing what God wanted me to do would last for another 9 years and cause lots more misery and lost opportunities.

My sometime Pioneer partner Mic was a strange soul. His father was the "Presiding Overseer" or "Head Elder" of our neighbouring congregation and I think he felt obliged to live up to his dads expectations. His brother was a high flyer in the Witnesses and even though he was dumb as a brick he was not a bad guy. Come to think of it his being dumb was probably the main reason why he was a high flyer!

I arrived at Mics home one morning only to be met by the angry face of his mother. "Abner wants to talk to you" she said sternly.

Now understand I liked Abner but he was a strange man speaking to him was very difficult, even more so as I was obviously in trouble. I walked into his study with a heavy heart.

"Neil. I am very disappointed in you." he said without warning. There's lots of stuff to be disappointed in so he'd have to narrow it down! Then he looked over at a large cardboard box sitting on a chair.

"Richard tells me that you have been storing these "Comic books" at our home because you are afraid your parents will find them."

I looked in the box without making it obvious and there was Mics precious "Secret" comic collection! For years now Mic had been collecting expensive graphic novels and hiding them in a caravan on the property! I could see his prized "Batman" books, his "Spawn" comic and even his demonic "Hell Raiser" books!

Now getting caught with these titles spelled a problem for Mic, he was a Pioneer! His father held a high position in the Hall so when confronted with the book he did what he thought was best, he blamed it on me!

I stood, paralysed while Abner ranted and read me verses from the Bible. Mic stood in the shadows whispering for me to take my beating like a man, I was fuming! So I did what I hope anyone would do in the same situation.

"You're right Abner" I said. "I'm so sorry to put you and your family in this position, I'm going to take these now and throw them away". I then took my new comic collection and walked 2 miles into town to sell them to the guy Mic had bought them from in the first place!

I few days later Mic came to my house to apologise for what had happened and to be reunited with his beloved collection, "You mean MY collection Mic" I said. "Your dad was right, those are terrible books. I threw them away for you". Poor Mics face was a picture of defeat and nearly made me feel sorry enough to give him the money I'd gotten but the life of a Pioneer is a hard one so I kept it instead.

It Must Be Me

There comes a time in the life of most Jehovah's Witnesses when you can't keep believing the lie. You have tried so hard to be a "Good Witness". Often for your entire life but then one little thing just pushes you over the edge and down you fall, your hopes and dreams along with you, into a black hole of despair and regret. There is still one tiny thread to hold on to and it is this, "but where else will you go to?" that is the stock phrase for all cult members. It allows you to stay in a terrible, toxic and claustrophobic cult even when you have become convinced that it is absolute crap!

From an early age, I was taught that all other religions were crooked, that they were not just wrong but that their worship actually angered Jehovah! We would drive past them on the way home from the Kingdom Hall,"Oh there's the once a week brigade" we'd say. We would laugh at Christians who couldn't argue their points, shake our heads knowingly when outgunned by someone who could and walk away saying "Satan has that poor man trapped". Whatever doubts we held about our own beliefs, we could always pretend that the other options were worse.

For Jehovah's Witnesses the whole point of faith and the cult itself, is the pursuit of truth. Not just truth but *"The Truth"* and so long as they can attach that name to whatever it is they currently believe then they are satisfied. I, for one, was determined to find the truth and place it under house arrest forever knowing exactly what it was and where it would be. Of course, real life is more complicated than this, truth is complicated and fluid. It's fluid for the Leadership of the Jehovah's Witnesses too so much so that they are very happy to alter what they believe if the alternative will cost them money or force them to admit that previous leaders were idiots but I digress.

We would often spend evenings at each others houses complaining bitterly about "Elder X" or "Sister Y". These conversations would carefully broach the dangerous waters of *Lake - Is This Religion Bullshit?* but, only just, as we were always nervous that talking would label any one of us a "Doubter" or even worse an "Apostate". Whatever was said the conversation would end up at the same point "Where else would you go to?". The answer was obvious, nowhere. It's obvious if you know nothing about other faiths except the lies and half truths fed to you by embittered liars in Brooklyn. If you knew more then the answer was equally obvious, ANYWHERE BUT HERE!

Once I left the Witnesses, I discovered that there are hundreds of faith and thousands of sub groups to chose from and almost all of them do more for others than the Jehovah' Witnesses. When I was younger and asked what charitable work we did for people involved in disasters I was told -

"We give them valuable literature" they said.

"But we don't give it to them, we sell it!" I replied.

They came back with "Gotta keep the lights on! Anyway, if you gave to people in need, you would never be sure that they didn't join for love of material things instead of love of Jehovah".

Imagine, someone so deeply flawed and unchristian that they think that's a reasonable view to hold, they must be crazy right? No one would ever teach something so terrible right?

Watchtower 1969 May 1 p.280

"If there is any material giving, to charities for instance, it is because there is need to salve a conscience, or because one's reputation is at stake."

Ohhhh!!. Well maybe that's "Old Light"? perhaps they think different-
ly now

Watchtower 2017May p.7

*"Like the neighbourly Samaritan in Jesus' illustration, we want to help
suffering people, including those who are not Witnesses. (Luke 10:33-37)
The best way to do so is by sharing the good news with them."*

*"It is important to make clear right away that we are Jehovah's Witnesses
and that our primary mission is to help them spiritually, not materially,"
notes an elder who has helped many refugees. "Otherwise, some may associate with us only for personal advantage."*

These, and many other reasons, made me question my beliefs again and
again but even if you become convinced that they're wrong there is another level of bullshit to get through before you escape! If, after years
and years of cult life, you get to the point where you just can't keep up
the pretence that what you believe is true, for you at least. So the cult
leaders have several nifty tricks up their sleeves to make the fault yours
and yours alone.

"You can't hack it" - Being a member of the one true religion is tough
work and you aren't up to the challenge! You might have spend a lifetime working for free to further its aims but if you came looking for
thanks during tough times you came to the wrong door! Pull your
socks up, get out on the preaching work and shut your mouth.

"The love of the greater number is cooling off" - Why the Bible
tells us that those who we once called Brother will lose the love they
once had, shame it had to be you. The Jehovah's Witnesses are already
primed to have the answers to your problems and they are YOUR
problems.

"They Are Perfect" - You are just picky and superior and think you know more than Jehovah's elected representatives on Earth. "How dare you think you know better than the Faithful and Discreet Slave Class!" they say. "You're not perfect, we know all your sins, we kept them in a folder at headquarters".

"They AREN'T Perfect" - Now, this argument is admittedly a little new to me. In my day suggesting that our mighty overlords weren't inspired by God would be grounds for a rushed excommunication or in very devout congregations possibly some sort of public flogging! But now they have turned things on their heads. Night is day and day is night and the Faithful and Discreet Slaves are really just lovely old men who may our may not be right on any occasion. It is the fact that we obey them anyway that really shows how much loyalty we have to God's Organisation!

On top of this awesome list of excuses for losing members we can also add the usual list of reasons, *"They were gay, Wanted to celebrate Christmas, Are Apostates"* and you can see that the modern Jehovah's Witness is well equipped to stay inside his cult bubble no matter who bursts out of their own. In fact, it's my experience that most Witnesses who leave their cult continue to believe almost all of what they were taught! These poor people go through life convinced that it's their fault! That one day they need to "Return To Jehovah" if they want to survive Armageddon which really is coming "any day now".

I speak to people stuck in this oddball half-life all the time. They have left their old life, gotten married and moved away but they still think that those old lies are true. The nonsense that is so easily disproved still holds power over them and whenever live gives them lemonade they put the blame on "Satan" and this "Wicked System Of Things". Too often they then head back to the Witnesses convinced that now they'll be safe. The fact that they are going back to a deeply flawed cult that has hidden countless child abusers and teaches lies so big they can blot out the sun, is entirely lost on them.

It was into this life that I cast myself at the age of 23 when I started to have real doubts about the Jehovah's Witnesses. I didn't stop going to the meetings entirely but I certainly slowed down a lot. Instead of regularly spending 20 hours a month on the Field Service I began to spent an Hour, or no time at all! Instead of attending the Assemblies and diligently taking notes, I arrived late and left early or left and went bowling! But whatever I did, I felt that it was MY fault. Jehovah was correct and who was I to question otherwise?

During this time, I began to experience the pleasure of being "Marked". Being "Marked" is really just an "In house" Disfellowshipping. The Elders know that you're up to no good but they can't really pin you down for any major sin and therefore the word is passed around that you are not a good Associate. I remember my mother telling me one day that friends of ours were having a fancy dress party and we had been invited, on the condition that I did not say anything negative about the Jehovah's Witnesses or the Elders. I was to be polite and shut my mouth. I arrived at party dressed as pop superstar, and all round sex symbol, Mark Bolan of T Rex. I chose him because I had lots of baggy blouses I could wear and we both shared a kinky Jew-fro hairstyle!

As per usual, the beers flowed and conversation turned to Witness matters. Over time people got closer and closer to revealing real gossip or criticizing Elders, I sat quietly as promised and drank my beer.

"I can't wait till the next Assembly, what do you think Neil?"

I sat and listened, thinking of a way to get out of a religious conversation that might get my part time shunning turned into a full time Disfellowshipping.

"Marc Bolan does not care about your religion. Marc Bolan only cares about Rock and Roll!" I said loudly. There was some quiet laughter, but most around me just thought that I had been drinking to much and I was left alone for the evening.

Like most other Jehovah's Witness men I knew, I had left school with no decent qualifications and so I was relegated to doing the one job that generations of Witness men had done before me. I became a Janitor! In particular, I became a self employed window cleaner, and once a part of this band of brothers I became trapped in it for a little under 25 years!

Even window cleaning wasn't immune from Elder scrutiny however. I wanted to expand my business and do bigger and better work, eventually get big commercial contracts and higher others. I was regularly reminded "There is great wisdom in keeping your eye simple Neil. If you spend your time building a business in these last days you'll have less time for the preaching work". I ignored this awesome advice and eventually had two employees and contracts with multi national companies and the my local City!

Generally though, I carried on as I had before, having moments of religious revival followed by depression and inactivity. I spent a fair bit of time in Southern Ireland visiting various friends. I remember one congregation I arrived at to attend a wedding. It was going to be one of those trips that really made you think hard about the Jehovah's Witness claims of being uniquely clean, of building better men.

I arrived at my friends house and was greeted by one of the local Elders, when I say greeted I really mean he walked up to me and gave me a warm hug. If it had stopped at a hug this story would be dull, but sadly he leant into me and tried to plant a less than brotherly kiss on my lips! Now, I'm not saying that this married father of four was gay but I do wonder why he found my youthful lips so dammed attractive that day!

As the weekend progressed I had my first experience with drugs! I had a small quantity of Marijuana which I smoked with another Jehovah's Witness from England. As we sat and smoked I still remember the words of wisdom he gave me.

"You're on the road to leaving the Truth Neil" he said seriously. "Trust me. I've been there and I can see it coming a mile away".

I smoked quietly and pondered whether or not I was in danger of leaving the narrow road that leads to Everlasting Life. Years later, I heard about that same brother, he had been convicted (again) of sexually abusing young girls in his Congregation. I heard his family and local Elders supported and defended him throughout the court case and while he was in prison. It turns out he was actually innocent! But Jehovah needed someone to go into prison and preach the Good News to dangerous paedophiles, so he had arranged for this job to be given to my old smoking partner. Last I heard, he had moved but is still knocking doors somewhere in Northern England.

So far in my religious life, I had sacrificed my school years to bullying and ostracism, nearly lost then actually lost my sister, left school with no qualifications straight into a (brief) career as door to door magazine salesman and my reward was to be pretty much ignored. Hell, I wasn't even trusted enough to read the Watchtower on a Sunday morning, maybe they had my card marked all along!

Around about the my own "End Times" among the Jehovah's Witnesses, I saw a perfect example of the power the Elders wielded in the congregations and the hypocrisy within our cult. It's also funny as hell, so let me tell you all about it!

I was going through, what I now see to be, the last of the "Peaks & Troughs" of my spiritual journey. At this point, I was really trying hard to improve my spirituality and get right with the congregation. I was attending a regular "Watchtower and Scrabble" sessions at an Elder friends house, held every Friday night and was going out on service regular as clockwork. I answered up at the meetings and when an Elder asked me what was responsible for my noticeable change I told him "I just try harder and harder every week. Every meeting I try to study deeper and deeper into the material so I can get the most out of it". That's right, I was going through an insufferable period.

It was at this time that a young Sister from Southern Ireland came to visit our Hall. Now, she was a bit older than I was and I genuinely had no interest in her but she did have an interest in another Brother, let's call him "David". Well, I knew David very well indeed! I knew what he did, how he spoke and exactly how little anyone would want their daughter to date him and filled with my rediscovered self righteous zeal I told her! I didn't go into details about what I knew him to be like but as I had never been taught to have a filter I left very little to the imagination. I honestly had only good intentions at the time, David was a truly shitty human and she ought to know it, so of course she told David immediately.

Unfortunately for me, David was also trying to turn over a new leaf and his journey was being personally guided by a very senior visiting Missionary Elder from Canada. This Elder took great offence to my warning young women off from his project and so I received a phone call from him and another Elder who informed me that they both wanted to see me at my parents house asap!

I obeyed as I was taught and despite nursing a broken foot from a car accident the week before stood at the front door waiting for them one Saturday afternoon.

These two Elders were, without a doubt, the most strict men in my Kingdom Hall. The Canadian Elder and his wife now claim to be members of the "Anointed Class" and have high hopes that they will rule over all mankind in the future. The other Elder was notoriously high handed and would soon be one of the main reasons I would leave the Jehovah's Witnesses, but for now I still treated both of them like the VIPs they were!

The first sign that things were wrong was the fact that despite seeing me standing there on my one unbroken foot, these two men proceeded to sit in their car reading and making notes for another 30 minutes. "Oh boy. I'm in trouble". I thought. I waited inside the house, until they decided I had stewed enough and then they knocked the door, came into the living room and got down to it.

"We have received some very troubling allegations Brother Gardner. We have heard that you are slandering the Brothers". The Elder asked.

"No I haven't". I replied. I told one Sister what I knew to be true about one other person.

"Well who gave YOU authority to speak on behalf of your congregation?" One asked. "Who do you think you are?"

"No one" I replied in full humble pie mode.

"I have been studying with David for many months now and he is CHANGED MAN!" Said the Missionary. He then hit me with the most pompous scriptural quotation in history.

"Who are YOU to say what is unclean when I have made it clean?" Here he was referring to the Biblical opening of the Christian message to non Jews in Acts 10:9-16 and applying it to his own transforming of David, from the reprobate I knew him to be, into the fine worshipper of Jehovah they knew and loved.

I would later learn that the Canadian Elder was likely a closeted homosexual who insisted on asking the victims in his Judicial Committees about the quantity and quality of the young men's seminal emissions. He also liked to take his "Projects" back to their homes after the meeting and discuss how often they had masturbated, so he was a totally normal guy then!

"Well I'm very sorry" I replied. "If you say he is a good man, I will never say another word against him". I never did say another word, in fact, I actually drove to his house, broken foot an all, to apologise to David and the Sister too. Such was the (brief) level of my obedience that I contritely begged them to forgive me and as good Christians of course they did, they even invited me to their wedding reception six months later...

They had invited lots of us to the wedding reception, so many in fact, that we borrowed a bus for the trip. The bus was driven by a local Elder called Pete. Pete worked for the company and we all met up at our Hall for the 45 drive to the venue. The bus Pete got us was huge and could only park at the back of the building but Pete was an expert driver and threw that thing around like a rally driver. We were just finishing the turn when the buses lights illuminated the back door and there was David.

He appeared to be practising, with some kind of ventriloquists dummy, well there must be some reasonable explanation for why he had is hand buried up the dress of a small woman. Sadly, there was a reason, he was right in middle of finding third base with the chief bridesmaid! Truth be told he was was well past third base and running hard towards home plate, Babe Ruth would have been proud. The entire bus watched as David stopped fingering the young lady and headed back inside. Nothing was ever said of the night although a marriage ended almost as soon as it began and David moved away very quickly.

Looking back on this story, what strikes me most is not the terrible choice that Sister made in a husband or even David's sadly typical behaviour, it was the fact, that despite both those Elders now knowing how wrong they had been about this excuse of a man. How intently they had bullied me (who was actually right on this occasion) neither of them bothered to, even quietly, apologise for their error.

I have looked out for David on Facebook once in a while, I have never found him, perhaps he's waiting for the dust to settle on the mound.

You're Worldly, I'm Not

You might not know this but you are not a good person, I mean, you might do good things, people may say nice things about. You may even think you have a good relationship with God but you are wrong, very very wrong. It is my sad task to tell you that you are not good (technically no one is) but especially not you, for you are a "Worldly" person, or even a "Worldling" if I want to be particularly rude about you! "But what is a worldly person and why is that even a bad thing" you say. I'm glad you asked, let me tell you all about it.

If you are not a Jehovah's Witness you are "Worldly" if you are worldly you can't be good! If someone is not an active Jehovah's Witness they're probably worldly and if they're worldly then you shouldn't associate with them, unless they are trying their absolute hardest to get back on track, in which case you can associate with them but you had better be careful!

The whole reason Jehovah's Witnesses exist is to make worldly people join their cult thereby becoming, hopefully, not-worldly. If you do that and then promise to obey their leaders in all things without complaining, doubting or refusing then you have the chance, possibly, potentially, maybe, of living forever in a paradise on earth, although you'll be sharing that earth with lots and lots of Jehovah's Witnesses which is probably not going to be a lot of fun but let's just stick to why you suck shall we?

You are not a good as Jehovah's Witnesses because you are NOT one. Because of that simple fact nothing you do will ever make you as good as them. As a child I remember going to the meetings and being encouraged, no not encouraged, threatened is a much better word, not to make friends with children in my school or neighbourhood. "The best worldly person isn't as good as the worst Witness" I was told. "Wow! These strange people must be really bad" I thought.

I can't tell you how many times I would be going out on service and see the huge houses and beautiful cars of the people I met. "When Armageddon comes I'm going to live there" I told myself, not once stopping to think that what I was actually doing was wishing the death of the owners and then making plans to move in afterwards like some ghoulish human vulture. I would love to tell you that I was the only sicko doing this but I'd be lying to you, loads of us picked out houses and cars for ourselves after mentally murdering the current keeper, but don't worry it's not wrong because they were worldly, see how this works?

At this point it would be fair to say that everything I've said so far would be denied by a Jehovah's Witness if you asked them about it, so let's hear it from their own lips instead!

Watchtower 2013 Feb study ed. p.24 "Our choice of associates. Of course, some contact with unbelievers — such as at school, at work, and when sharing in the ministry — is unavoidable. It is quite another matter, though, to socialize with them, even cultivating close friendships with them. Do we justify such association by saying that they have many good qualities? "Do not be misled," warns the Bible. "Bad associations spoil useful habits." (1 Cor. 15:33) Just as a small amount of pollution can contaminate clean water, friendship with those who do not practice godly devotion can contaminate our spirituality and lead us into adopting worldly viewpoints, dress, speech, and conduct."

So non Witnesses are a pollutant, they are worse than blue-green Algae in a lake at the end of summer! They spoil good habits and close contact should be avoided, I bet they never told you that the last time they knocked on your door!

Watchtower 2010 Sep 15 p.14 *"The spirit of companionship that unites those who work together in God's service is far stronger than the spirit that unites others in the world who merely socialize together."*

I love this one! Jehovah's Witnesses are united, they are a band of brothers, worldly people merely "Socialize", don't tell your mum that!

Awake 1996 October 22 p.15 *"Since worldly people are existing as slaves of corruption, their company cannot bring you true happiness."*

You're a slave, nuff said.

Watchtower 1987 September 15 p.12 Breathing This World's "Air" Is Death-Dealing!

*"While, **some contact with worldly people is unavoidable**-at work, at school, and otherwise-we must be vigilant so as to keep from being sucked back into the death-dealing atmosphere of this world.... Let the world go along in its way, reaping its bad fruitage in the form of broken homes, illegitimate births, sexually transmitted diseases, such as AIDS, and countless other emotional and physical woes."*

If worldly people don't get AIDS now they soon will and we all know that people with AIDS should be shunned, not hard since they probably live in a cardboard box anyway also, your dad is not really your dad, sorry about that.

Dating And Haste to Mate

"Thousands of young Christian men and women are willingly sacrificing marriage or are not having children—at least for now—in order to serve Jehovah to the full." **Watchtower 2016 Apr Study ed. p.9**

Looking back on my teenage days as a Jehovah's Witness, I can tell you that a lot of my time was spent looking at girls. I am told that this is also true (though opposite) for most girls too! For most teenagers the choice of prospective partners is pretty wide. What with family friends, neighbours, members of any club you belong too and of course church and school they have a lot of options, for us it was a little different.

For a Jehovah's Witness kid the pool was a bit more shallow. In fact, don't think of it as a pool at all. Instead I want you to imagine one of those shallow muddy swamps you see in nature programs and instead of the bright and healthy carp the worldly kids got to pick from, think of those weird goggle eyed little mudskippers and crusty frogs.

In our dried up puddle even a tiny fish would fascinate us, "Oh my god, look at her, she's got gills!" "He's got fins!".

The possibility that there existed a match for us, that wasn't intolerable in at least three different ways, was pie in the sky. For the record I'm not suggesting that I was some kind of beautiful flower! It takes a strong stomach to wake up to me every morning and I thank God every day I found someone willing to take the job on! In fact, I was even less of a catch back then! What with my spotty face, curly hair that could only be contained in a Jew-fro style and my doughy body I hardly made for the ideal love match!

For Jehovah's Witness kids however there were many real and invented problems that came up as you looked around in search of a boyfriend or girlfriend, let's have a look at some of them.

1. You must get married quickly or not date at all!

For Jehovah's Witness kids dating is not a recreational activity. For them dating has a single purpose and that is to find a wife or husband. I doubt there is a single Jehovah's Witness who, when dating a girl was asked "Are you dating with a view to marriage Brother?" this question, usually asked by some pompous ass desperate for promotion in the Kingdom Hall was supposed to bring your mind back to one of the main teachings of the Witnesses and the quote at the beginning of this chapter "DON'T GET MARRIED".

For Witnesses, marriage was only to be entered into if you could not control your body members (your junk, just to be clear!). So if you simply couldn't function due to your chronic masturbation, then it was acceptable (just) to find a wife to satisfy your urges. Needless to say, these marriages born out of "Haste to Mate", as a good friend of mine christened it, were often doomed to failure since neither person knew the other well, let alone themselves. They married simply because the prospect of a sexless life was to awful and so they jumped into a union with the first person they met and suffered the consequences.

2. You need to choose someone who is "Spiritually Mature"

So what does being "Spiritually Mature" mean? Well, to put it simply, you must only date a person if you, your family and local Elders consider them to be a person "Strong in the Truth". To be "Strong in the Truth", you need to have shown that you are a serious and obedient Witness. They need to show that they are keen to advance and gain promotion in the Kingdom hall or, if a lady, they need to show that they are demure and obedient.

The sharp eyed reader will notice that I never mentioned that your future partner had to be good looking or satisfy you intellectually, that's because all the normal things you look out for in a partner are not only unimportant they are ignored!

I knew a lovely girl (let's call her Janice) in my old kingdom hall. She was about 19 when I left the cult, a few years later I stood outside the Hall during a funeral to show my respects for an older lady who had died and I saw Janice again, as she guided her elderly husband into the hall. She held his left hand and he held a walking stick with his other,. This young woman was tall, pretty and smart and yet in her teens she had married an elderly man who was "Spiritually Mature", I bet the sex is dynamite.

3. Most young people leave or are kicked out of the Jehovah's Witnesses

The choice of partner for a Witness teen is also very limited. They can't date or marry "Outside the Truth", so they only have a tiny group to choose from. If I had to give you an example I'd ask you to imagine a food counter in the former Soviet USSR. The queue was long and slow and the food available was poor and limited so when you got to the front of the line it seemed natural to grab whatever was left and take it home with you, this is how I managed to date when I was younger!

We've already covered the fact that you may have to date and eventually marry a man or women who is older than your parents but even if you do find someone your won age it's quite likely.

4. Most young people who stay are mental!

You have grown up in a cult that quietly encourages your parents to beat the living shit out you for being a child. You have been taught that masturbation is a terrible sin and you need to stop it. You have few, if any, normal friends and you have given up any chance at a decent education or career but that's not all! For a man to make it in "The Truth" he has to be more interested in getting along inside it than getting along with his wife! If you're a woman you need to be quiet, obedient and docile, so remember to throw those short skirts in the bin ladies!

Any quick look, or even a long hard look through your local Kingdom Hall will reveal a plethora of lunatics, fanatics, janitors, hypochondriacs and that small group of people, or ones just like them in a congregation not far away are what you get to chose from for a partner. Not just for now, but for the rest of both of your potentially eternal lives! If I am driving a car for more than a week, I think very carefully about what I'm picking but in his wisdom Jehovah had decided that all you need is a poorly educated window cleaner with a tenth grade education and the views of a medieval king, lucky you!

How To Be A Bad Human

I have read a LOT of ex-cult member memoirs on Scientology, Charismatic Christians, Mormons and (Of course) Jehovah's Witness but one thing they all usually share is a sense that the during their time inside, the author had an unbelievable level of holiness. A massive unswerving dedication to their beliefs that made them an example to others throughout the years right up until the day they left. Now, I don't doubt that they all had their moments, I know I did, but I believe it's impossible to hold to the rigorous and often impossible standards that were set for us.

I believe that even if we were able to somehow walk that finest of lines it is the very walking it that forces us to fail and eventually produces sub par human beings.

I can see why us writers will seek to pretend that we were a unique and special flower, that we were different from the others. For one it allows the writer to concentrate as much writing time and effort as possible doing what we intended, exposing the cult that we have left. Secondly, it can be difficult to admit that not only were you foolishly living inside a cult for many years but you were also kind of an asshole and that fact doesn't change entirely just because you left! Thirdly, it's tough to attack other peoples failures whilst frankly admitting your own. I think if you try you'll actually be living up to the old parable about removing the rafter in your own eye before pointing out the splinter in the eyes of other people. You'll be true to your own experience and tell a story that will resonate with others and you'll be able to hold your head up when it's done. So that's what I'm trying to do!

In my experience, Jehovah's Witnesses go through fits and starts where we are enthusiastic members and then miserable rule breakers. We usually feel pretty good when we're breaking the rules but our conditioned guilt then hits us hard and we try to revive our spirituality. Even today, I speak to former Witnesses who have been out for many years and they live with a crippling guilt for simply living as normal people. They feel that missing meetings and not preaching to others is such a severe sin that they must get back to it "One day". It's incredibly common for ex-Witnesses to talk about their collective past and reveal the most shocking secrets about people each thought were fine and upstanding examples of Christian men and women, such is the see saw life of us cult members!

I'm convinced that the best and most zealous looking Jehovah's Witnesses have just been able to hide their periods of sinning and inactivity better than I did. By pretending they were always serious people, they ended up getting coveted promotions even though they had very little ability or interest in helping others. They end up keeping the whole show going even though no-one can live by its rules or even enjoys trying. I really did believe what I was taught and even though I failed and spent months at a time trying my best to do as little as possible. I also experienced those rare highs when I thought that what I was doing what was right, that was when I was at my most dangerous as I usually looked for the same level of intensity from others and God help them if they couldn't live up to it!

So far I haven't really gotten into what kind of man comes out of a cult. A young boy or girl, gets pushed from birth into their cult sausage maker and eventually comes out the other end a fully developed man or woman but what sort of man or woman do they become? The Jehovah's Witnesses will tell you that living as a Witness and learning their unique teachings will make you a better man, a better husband and produce better happier families but is that true?

Not as far as I can see and I'll tell you why. The very qualities you need to possess to be a good and obedient cult member make you unsuitable to qualify as a normal person afterwards but wait it gets worse! The qualities you need to develop throughout your life to be considered a *successful* cult member and gain respect and promotion will almost certainly make you a thoroughly terrible person and here's why.

Let's say you have a friend who tells you a secret. Their husband hit them while drunk and in a moment of madness they took comfort in a workmates arms and made love to them, what would you do?

Well, if you're the sort of friend the Jehovah's Witnesses make, you'll go straight to the local Elders and report your friend and maybe the husband. Her sinful behaviour will then be dealt with by a committee of older men who will decide if she is to be excommunicated for adultery. If they go ahead with this punishment, which is very likely, you'll cheerfully shun her until the Elders decide she has repented of her sin and allow her to rejoin the cult.

The damage this course of action will have on her life, her children's lives and your relationship won't be an issue because you have been taught to do your duty, even if doing it causes irreparable harm to everyone around you. Congratulations! you're a shitty friend and a terrible human being.

Now, let's say you have a new buddy who is a bit effeminate, he might even be a closet homosexual. He's a great guy and really trying hard to get on in his new cult life, even though they really dislike gays. He has had a very tough life, his family have completely abandoned him because he joined the Jehovah's Witnesses. He has mental health problems because of this but now he feels he's part of a new family and seems happy.

Now imagine that you are at his house one day and accidentally discover a letter he's written to a classified ad looking for new members to join a gay support group, what do you do? Well if you're a good cult member you run to the Elders (starting to see a pattern?) and tell them all about it. The fact that he will certainly be excommunicated and left completely alone won't even pass through your head as you spill the beans and then run away like a coward.

Now comes the bit where I admit my own flaws, I did that last one. I reported that my friend was gay and that was the end of our relationship and his new "family". He was shunned and moved away. To be fair to me, I did approach him first to tell him what I had done. I still remember the look of horror and shame in his face as he screamed "You shouldn't have done that Neil" and then he ran out into the night. No, I shouldn't and I still feel bad about it to this day.

The point I'm getting at with these two stories is that personal relationships, secrets and sins are all subject to the rule of the Elders. You MUST tell them if you know something that you feel they ought to know. Failure to do this will make you just as guilty as the original sinner and even more likely to be excommunicated since your sin is one that required conscious effort. The fact that you cannot keep a confidence spills over into every aspect of your life.

I remember a young guy in my hall "Paul", he was a Pioneer and "Ministerial Servant". One sad day he let booze get the better of him at a concert and drunkenly interrupted a live news report from outside the venue.

Reporter – "So why do you like the supergroup Oasis?"

Young Women (Also a Jehovah's Witness from my hall) – "Well, I...."

"Paul - Because they've all got big willies!" Paul is dancing wildly and jumping front of the camera.

Reporter – "Back to the studio."

The next day Paul was inconsolable, It's not often that you screw up so badly and so publicly! My brother and I arrived at his apartment to both laugh at and comfort Paul. We got him to calm down and he told us that he was to see the Elders later that day. So I started to give him advice.

"Tell them how sorry you are. Throw yourself on their mercy" I said. "Tell them you realize that you have fallen in with a bad crowd, call them bad associates and it has damaged your spirituality. Tell them you'll stop it now and get back on track."

Paul agreed to do just that and thanked us before he left to meet his fate. I came back that evening to collect a guitar I'd left at his home but when I pushed the buzzer all I got was a "I'll be a second, I'm on my way down."

Paul opened the door but wouldn't let me in. "What's wrong?" I asked.

"Well I told the Elders what you said Neil......But I told them you were the bad associate". He then slammed the door in my face and as I stood outside shouting for my guitar he tossed it out the window. We Jehovah's Witnesses are such bad human beings that we are willing to dump friends and relatives for the sake of inconvenience but that's not all, let's get back to my failures!

Years later, when talking to an old friend of mine, I mentioned that Paul was now a Sr Missionary serving in Brazil. My friend looked amazed and asked in amazement "Who is he a missionary for, the Jehovah's Witnesses?".

When I was about 20 and working briefly, for a firm of accountants. A group of co-workers asked me to leave with them to start up a rival firm. Sadly, we were overheard and reported to the owner. I still remember standing in a line with my co-conspirators as the boss asked us what we had been talking about.

"Sports" said friend one.

"Yup, sports" replied friend two.

"Neil is this true?" the owner asked me.

Now, I had been taught to never lie and to obey those in authority. The very IDEA that I could simply not answer a question when asked it was one I had never been taught. I would have cheerfully reported on my own parents sins if I felt obliged to do so, so it won't come as a surprise to learn what I said.

"Well...friend one wants to leave and start a rival firm. Friend two is funding it through a re-mortgage on his home and they both want me to join as a junior partner if I can find £5,000.00".

This spilling of my guts felt so natural and so normal that I couldn't understand why both men were looking at me as I if I had pissed on the floor. The older of the two just stood their shaking his head and smiling. They were both kept on and the owner had no choice but to give them a raise. I got kicked out pretty soon after. The guys left anyway and set up their new business, it's doing very well even decades later, they did not need a junior partner.....

The story of ex-cult members is often very similar. Bullied at school, picked on by teachers, ignored by cult leaders, treated badly by friends and family and eventually they leave or are shunned but why is it the same story? Well, if you were anything like me it's because you were insufferable!

Looking back I see that I was bullied because I told on kids in class constantly, smugly informed them that Santa wasn't real and had no idea what things other kids liked because I was so bloody odd! I was picked on by teachers because when I refused to take part in hundreds of different quasi religious activities I wasn't "Bravely standing up for Jehovah". I was being awkward and painting a target on my back that I could never remove. I was ignored by fellow cult members who were even more screwed up than I was because they had been a part of the whole system much longer than me.

I left because I couldn't walk that line anymore. No matter how hard I tried, I couldn't walk it once I knew that it was all a lie anyway and when I came out into the world I remained a fairly terrible person who was incapable of being a good friend to anyone or even a good person, but I'm getting better I promise!

When you leave a cult, any cult, you have to remake yourself. You have to start from the bottom up and build a normal person. If you're lucky, you'll have some parts relatively normal already because you picked stuff up from family or friends. Unfortunately many don't and there's nothing so sad as to hear about people who leave the Jehovah's Witnesses and carry on thinking how they were taught to behave will get them through life successfully, because it really won't. I know many people who have ended up with mental illness, drug or alcohol addiction or going from one failed relationship after the next because they thought that they understood what they should do and how they needed to live.

In my final chapter, I'll go into what you can do to help remake yourself if you feel the need. Whether you do or not, the act of questioning your beliefs and assumptions is important and will help you. Too many people learn that they have been taught a lie and then disgusted and shocked they leave the Jehovah's Witnesses forever but they never consider what those lies built. It's looking at them in the mirror and, if I'm anything to go by, he's kind of a dick.

Post Script

I contacted my old friend a few years ago on Facebook to apologise for outing him and causing him so much hurt and he was enormously kind. He forgave me without making me squirm and told me that leaving was the best thing he ever did as It would never have worked "What with the whole poofter thing".

Neil Gets Creative

The following is a poem I performed at the Crescent Arts Centre in Belfast. If you would like to see me reading it that evening here is a link to my YouTube channel https://www.youtube.com/watch?v=34kcPn-jGq-c&t=29s

I was born special, a chosen son, gonna live forever when the kingdom comes.

Brought up happy, happiest of all, but always scared in case I should fall.

Loved by my parents but missed so much, like birthdays, Easter, Christmas and such.

Went to school but never had friends, cause they'd all be dead come the end.

Preaching to my neighbours, like a fool, every Monday morning came abuse in school.

Bullied and beaten, humiliated by teachers. Par for the course when you're a 10 year old preacher.

But it was all worth it because I served GOD all other religions were just fraud.

Yet at church I never felt the love, despite all those promises from god above.

You see my church asked more than others, If you wanted the privilege of being called a brother.

You had to learn "THE TRUTH".... about Jehovah god, whether he was 1, 2, 3 or quad.

Protected from others because they were bad, believed every word since it came from dad.

We had our own school, which was uncool, where we learned dumb rules, as a little kid I gave talks on a stepping stool. Parents were proud but we were all fools, suffered under misrule, kingdom hall was a cesspool forbidden from even going to a trade school.

University was a great sin if you tried to go you got lots of spin. Elders said you were holding on by thin skin in fact your actions were akin, to Apostasy.

See, Apostasy is not a good place to be. It meant you had betrayed god because your mind was flawed. The elders descended in a great squad to tell you why you were a lousy sod, perhaps you're odd?

Instead you should do some outreach, by this they meant preach, door to door without cease, taking from society like a leach....until you're to old to do your bit.

Till you lost the grit and have to quit.

But then you're old, no kids no gold. Living in a 1 room flat.

No visits, See if you can't make church they forget you and leave you in the lurch, unless you backtrack and do some research first.

Find out who made you and what things they'd do. Learn about the failed predictions which were only fictions.

Read about your leaders, who'd quote the bible in selected chunks but were really just abject drunks, maybe visit JW Facts who debunk....

Their lies when they make you sing "keep your eyes on the prize"

"They fuck you up your mum and dad", was the start of a poem I had. What I didn't know was that in my church it should read,

"We'll fuck your kids" which I heard the bible definitely forbids. Then laugh when lives are ruined and hit the skids. hide the crime so the pervert never does time and honestly this stuff is just too sad to rhyme,

15 years ago I left through a trail of tears....and it still fucks me up. They were my mum and dad too. They even told me "I love you"

So now you're out, in Babylon the great, if you want saved, sorry mate to late, your a rotten limb and they amputate.

Just wait cause you'll have a bad fate, date a bad mate,

your life will detonate unless you return prostrate, cause that's just how they operate.

IT'S NOT TRUE! IT'S A LIE. You'll meet a stand up guy, who sees eye to eye, becomes your ally.

In years to come you'll be at a black tie thinking about the outcry when you said goodbye to a cult that used you and abused you and I hope this poem gives you something to chew too.

They played me for a fool, don't let them do the same to you.

Thank You Al Gore!

Al Gore is sometimes claimed to be the inventor of the Internet, that's not true, but if it were he would be responsible for the two greatest things in my life, let me tell you about them.

So after more than two and a half decades of (semi) loyal service to Jehovah I was still going to the meetings and dragging myself from door to door. For sure, I was had lost a lot of my enthusiasm for the whole thing but as I just said in the last chapter, "If I left where would I go to?". I had decided that the answer was "nowhere" and had resolved myself to just do what I needed to do to get by. Perhaps in the next few years I'd find a girl, settle, get married, have kids and surely that would make life worthwhile, even if my spiritual life was unfulfilling and depressing.

I can confidently tell you that this is exactly what would have happened if it was not for two lucky breaks at this point. One was finally leaving my parents house and the other was the invention of the Internet, which Al Gore famously claimed to have invented, hence the title of this chapter!

At 25, it's fair to say that I wasn't the fastest bird to leave the nest. Eventually, even I moved out and into a small one bedroom apartment in Lisburn, just a few miles away from my mum and dad and even closer to the Kingdom Hall. At the urging of a friend, I bought a cheap personal computer and joined the miracle that is the Internet.

Back then the Internet was dial up and much of my free time was spent waiting for hours as naked pixilated women gradually appeared on my screen in ever clearer detail! Let me tell you, for an innocent virgin whose experience with naked girls was largely limited to walking in on his sister aged five during a camping trip and shouting "I seen your boobies" this was a culture shock!

It wasn't the naked ladies that caught my attention when I first went online though, it was an internet message forum called H20. It was dedicated to talking about Jehovah's Witnesses, the good the bad and the ugly and to me that was amazing! I first went on to H20 thinking that I would meet up with other Witnesses, possibly make some friends, meet a girl, get married, have kids, enjoy a happy meaningful life, so no pressure then! At this point in my life I had gotten so low that I had been placed on anti depressants by my doctor.

My work life as a lowly window cleaner was the same as it always was but my relations inside the Kingdom Hall had deteriorated. Due to my questioning nature I had been "Marked" by quite a few people. Basically this meant that gossip had gotten around the Hall that I was up to no good, which was quite mean since I was spending most of my time trying to justify all the cruel actions that I saw in the Kingdom Hall day in day out. I may have missed more meetings than I should have but I was spending that time trying to convince myself that I was in the right place and doing what God wanted me to do.

The first time I clicked onto H20 I sat shocked. This wasn't a forum for Jehovah's Witnesses it for a forum for ex Jehovah's Witnesses, Apostates! I was horrified! You see, I had always known about this rare thing known as an Apostate but to the best of my knowledge, there were only a tiny number and they were too busy indulging in gay sex and Satanic worship to go on the internet. So, what was happening here?

I looked around and saw literally hundreds of members, all ex Witnesses, all talking to one another, TALKING TO EACH OTHER! Any decent person knows that once you leave the Witnesses, you don't talk to other ex Witnesses and you certainly don't form a community to discuss your experience. Yet, that is exactly what these people were doing and to make matters worse they were making fun of their former religion, MY religion! The proper thing for a disfellowshipped person to do was to sit alone in a room feeling sad and studying the Watchtower while thinking about what they did wrong to get disfellowshipped in the first place.

As I sat looking on in disgust, they told mean jokes about the Elders in their former Halls, insulted them, SWORE when talking about them! They actually mocked the Governing Body of Jehovah's Witnesses, our supreme spiritual leaders and they didn't stop there. They talked about what teachings we had wrong, like refusing to celebrate birthdays, salute the flag, join the military or vote. They told stories about what made them leave and they didn't seem in the least bit sad or repentant and not a single one of them was trying to return, this was madness!.

The thing that really upset me, stopped my binge reading and forced me to actually comment on the site was a post by a member called Farkel. In it he made jokes about a belief that was very close to my heart, our refusal to eat blood or take blood transfusions. As you know my family had been put in this horrible situation when my sister Karen was hit by a car, so to see somebody making light of what was quite literally, a life or death situation, made my blood boil. With trembling hands I commented and even though, nearly two decades has passed, I still remember my reply to his post like it was yesterday. It was called "A Letter To Farkel" and though I thought it a fine piece of Christian apologetics, back then it was really just an angry scream! I'll try to recreate it for you.

Dear Farkel,

Why are you writing these lies about Jehovah? You **KNOW** we are right about blood transfusions. You **KNOW** we are right about the New System! Don't insult the Governing Body, they are Jehovah's representatives on Earth!

If we're so bad where else would you go to? (yes that old chestnut) Why are you saying these things? You must be very bitter.

Come back to the meetings. The end is coming soon and you'll be destroyed at Armageddon unless you do.

Signed

Josephus

(That was the name I went by back then)

As you can see, this was a cutting edge argument and bound to make anyone doubting "The Truth" come back to their senses immediately, amazingly that's not the way it turned out!

To say that my heartfelt letter did not get the reception I expected is an understatement. Think of a car park outside a fast food outlet just as someone throws away food. From out of a clear blue sky birds descend, every last one screeching "Mine, Mine, Mine" and tearing the food to pieces. That is more or less what happened to me. Except, I was the food and those terrible Apostates were the birds!

"Who is this idiot?"

"Is he joking? Oh God I hope so"

"Did you know that you've been predicting Armageddon for over 100 years?"

"Did you know a member of the Governing Body resigned because he found out it's all a lie, he wrote a book you know/"

"Did you know your founder is buried under a giant pyramid?" (This is actually a lie, he's buried BESIDE a giant pyramid which is totally different).

"You're brainwashed!"

I was mocked by so many people, in so many different and humiliating ways, that even now it stings a little to think about it. I honestly couldn't read half the replies without feeling as if I'd been beaten up and left for dead, but the one that hurt me the most was from Farkel himself.

Josephus,

The bible teaches that blood is to be poured out on the ground as a symbol of the sanctity of life. If someone uses it to save a life, wouldn't that be an even better use of blood? If a person does die because they refused blood wouldn't they be treating the symbol of life as more more important than an actual life?.

I was stunned.

Our refusal to take blood transfusions, however messy it had gotten regarding the use of blood "Fractions" by that point, was one of the main teachings that I believed. With one short reply this Apostate had filled my head with doubts. I tried to reply, after all I had to defend my faith to all men, the Jehovah's Witnesses taught me that! So I answered several of these wicked bullies and sat back feeling a lot more nervous than I thought I would. I had the stupid idea that the action of bravely standing up to these bullies would send them back to their internet caves but it wasn't working out that way!

Once again I received an internet smack down.

"Did you know the Witnesses supported Hitler?" one person asked.

"Did you know Rutherford (the second leader of the Witnesses) was a drunk?".

"Did you know they allowed Brothers to die in Africa over a small issue but allowed Brothers in Mexico to pay bribes to pretend they were in the Army?".

"What about 1975? they said the world would end".

Written punches flew at me from left, right, up and down. I'm pretty sure a few even came from a different dimension! but it left me with absolutely zero credibility and I knew it. The current leadership of the Jehovah's Witnesses might have arguments to reduce the damage these comments did to me but since they refused to acknowledge that there were criticisms, I was in no position to fight back and I was forced to do some thinking.

I had always held a huge amount of love and respect for the leaders of our religion, The Governing Body. Sure they changed from time to time but I had always been led to believe that they were the most honest and decent men you would find anywhere. I went to see one speak once, Milton Henchsell I think, and though his talk was quite boring, I went along with the general feeling of awestruck cheerfulness. It was like the Pope was visiting Ireland, only he was in a boxing arena. Nobody, but a few thousand people cared but to me it was a great trip to Dublin and I needed to ask permission to go, so I was honoured to be there!

It was this respect that made me really curious about the comment that one person had made,

"Did you know a member of the Governing Body resigned because he found out it's all a lie? he wrote a book you know".

This couldn't be true? Who was it and why hadn't I heard about this? I thought. So, I did something I never intended to do, I decided to ask the Apostates a question. I had only ever intended to do a drive by attack on these people, I never actually wanted to engage them!

First of all it was forbidden! they were mentally diseased and I didn't want whatever sickness they had rubbing off on me. Secondly, I never thought I'd need to actually have a conversation with them! The truth about the Witnesses was self evident, all I ever wanted to do was shine a light on the cockroaches and watch them scurry away. It was not working out like that, the cockroaches had climbed up my leg and were whispering in my ear and what they were saying was not good. So, with great reluctance I made this comment.

Dear Farkel, who on the Governing Body wrote and book and where can I get it?

To his credit Farkel replied, but not before a dozen enthusiastic others answered too!

His name is Raymond Franz and he left the Witnesses years ago after deciding that it was wrong. They tried to make him keep quiet but he wrote a book about it. It's called *"Crisis Of Conscience"* you can buy it on Amazon

This answer gave me even more questions! "What is an Amazon and why does it sell books?".

Finding out the answer to this led me to discover that the internet had more uses than just watching pictures of naked ladies and talking to Apostates, you can buy books too! I have always had the greatest love for reading, I devoured all the Witness literature and then anything else I could get. I went to a pretty rough school so used to hide library books under my coat in case my classmates caught me reading! It was this love that made me consider buying and reading an Apostate book so that's just what I did, I went to Amazon and ordered *"Crisis Of Conscience"*.

I had it sent to my parents house as I had never ordered anything to be delivered before. The problem with that was that my parents were loyal Witnesses and would go through the roof if they opened the parcel, so I told my mum that a book was arriving and it was about running a business or something else boring and then I waited for it to arrive! A few days passed and the book arrived. My mum called me to let me know and I drove up as fast as I could, snatching it from her hands like I had ordered a bag of heroin. I went home, closed the blinds and carefully opened the book.

Every once in a while, you will open a book and discover, much to your own surprise, that you are completely unable to close it. This doesn't happen often but when it does you find yourself sitting up late at night, fixated on what you're reading, walking with a book in one hand and your dinner plate in the other always trying to find a moment to read just one more page, that's how it was for me. *"Crisis Of Conscience"* is a big book and it's not really an easy read. It was written by an elderly man whose previous work (The Watchtower magazine) is hardly known for being unputdownable but this book was just that, it was epic! Every page taught me something new and often left me horrified. Every chapter was filled with facts that I have never heard, never even suspected and I spent hours lost in amazement and just as many hours with tears running down my face.

I approached my brother Steven to tell him about what I had read and he was worried and sceptical. It's funny but such is the power of cult mind control that my own brother (never a very devout Witness) felt it vital to warn me. "Neil" he said urgently. "You're falling into Satan's Trap! That's how he gets you!" I had indeed fallen for facts and those are hard to ignore!

The final straw for me during this time was handed to me by an Elder in my hall. James was a "Hard Line Elder". He was constantly getting into people privates lives, handing out unwanted advice and generally annoying everyone. He loved nothing more than instigating unnecessary investigations into young people and then punishing them for imagined sins.

I had first met James when he moved to Lisburn from Southern Ireland, he had moved his family up to my part of the world after falling out with the Elders down there. It's always a bad sign if a new Witness moves into your hall and immediately tells you "I had to move, Jehovah's spirit wasn't there". It's a strange fact that, even though I doubt Jehovah's spirit resides in any Kingdom Hall, you can be certain that anyone who uses that line is almost certainly an idiot.

James made waves as soon as he moved to Lisburn. He began training to become a doctor, not a real doctor of course, that'd take a lot of effort. Instead James decided to become the Jehovah's Witness version, that's right a medicine man.

At first he learned the ancient art of Reflexology, then Japanese Zuno medicine. After that solid grounding in science, he took up Kinesiology and began telling anyone who would listen that simply by applying pressure to your outstretched arms he could tell you were lying to him or not. You can see that at this point James was really developing an impressive set of skills! So what did my congregation Elders do with such a man? That's right, they made him an Elder.

Now James and I had a difficult relationship. At one point he had used me to investigate everyone I knew, his inquisition had the effect of convincing about 6 people to quit the Jehovah's Witnesses and left me friendless for a long time. We fell out in time after I stubbornly refused to play along with his medical quackery and laughed when he tried to push my arms down and claim I was lying, after that James decided I was a bad associate and he made it clear to me that he was just waiting for me to screw up so he could get me.

The last time I saw James at a meeting was on a Thursday evening. My brother Steven and I had gone to the hall alone that night and sat together. Towards the end of the last talk Steven whispered something to me and James (sitting in front of us) turned around and loudly said "Shush!" Now it sounds silly now but to be told off publicly by an Elder is a terrible thing! The whole hall went quiet, even the man giving the talk stuttered and then carried on quietly.

Steven leant over and whispered once again (He also on James hit list!) "Let's leave as the last prayer is ending, I don't want to get into an argument with that man". I was about to reply when once again James turned around, raised himself up to his feet and shouted "I SAID KEEP QUIET!"

Well this time the hall stopped dead! In my 25 years as a Witness I had never experienced anyone shouting in the Kingdom Hall and this time the person shouting was an Elder, AT ME!

I was momentarily stunned until I heard another voice beside me say "Sit down you obnoxious man". My brother had just told off an Elder, IN THE KINGDOM HALL! This would be enough to finish off nearly anyone and I couldn't let him stand alone. I scrunched all my courage together and in a shaky voice said "See me about this outside after the meeting James".

We still left as the meeting ended since I had no intention of actually confronting this bully, I had been only temporarily brave but inside I was still a coward! Both Steven and I waited for the inevitable backlash. We knew that standing up for yourself was a no-no and trouble was coming but by now both Steven and I were less indoctrinated than before. We had seen and experienced years of abuses and just weren't interested in bowing down to these men anymore.

The news arrived that James was calling for a full Judicial Committee against me. I had, he alleged, "Called him outside for a fist fight during the meeting" and I needed to be dealt with immediatley. I did the only thing I could, I went to see Roland who was an Elder I trusted to see what I should do but I didn't go alone, I carried with me my copy of "*Crisis Of Conscience*"!

You may remember Roland from an earlier chapter, it was he who was instrumental in forcing my parents to kick my sister out of her home. It was him who disfellowshipped her in the first place! Strangely and despite all this Roland and I were close friends. We had gone rock climbing and mountaineering together for many years and I felt able to speak freely both to him and to his wife Vera. Both were incredibly intelligent people and had given up the chance of bright futures to become full time preachers for the Jehovah's Witnesses.

I went to their home that day to talk about the supposed "Threats" I made but also to throw myself on their mercy. We covered the nonsense quite quickly and I knew Roland had my back, he had always disliked James and I believe seriously regretted that he was ever made an Elder, so then I started to say the main reason why I was there. "I am really sorry Roland" I said. I want to talk to you about a book I just read. I know I shouldn't have but I did and it's really shaken my faith". I took the book out and of a bag and handed it to Roland.

Both Roland and Vera looked at me with real sadness and then Roland replied, "Neil. We are very disappointed in you. You should not have read this book"..... "However we love you like our own son and so we'll read it and tell you where it's lying". I thanked them both, we hugged and I went home.

I returned a few days later to find a very grim Roland and Vera waiting for me.

"Well, did you read the book?" I asked nervously.

"We did Neil, it's all a lie." Vera replied.

"Oh good" I sighed.

"No Neil" said Roland. "It's a lie. We have lived a lie for most of our lives. Everything in that book is true and we can't be a part of this religion anymore".

We talked for hours and I learned that my worst fears were true. The religion I had grown up in, had given my heart and soul to, was a complete lie. I was both excited and heartbroken.

True to their word Roland quickly finished up with his outstanding duties as an Elder and both he and Vera stopped going to the meetings but not before they began to tell others about what they knew! Because of their activism 3 more families left the Witnesses and the Watchtower Society was forced to deal with the "Apostates of Lisburn". Families were moved into the area and members told to never mention it again. I took this as my opportunity to quit too and I never returned!

I left the cult of Jehovah's Witnesses when I was 25 years old but it never really left me. I kept busy working two jobs but suffered from pretty serious depression as a result of leaving the Witnesses. At one point I considered suicide as I couldn't imagine that I'd ever find a way to fit into life outside "The Truth". I didn't officially quit though, I'd need to write a resignation letter for that, my parents were still loyal Witnesses and I didn't want them to be forced to shun me like they had my sister Karen all those years before. Instead, I kept my head down and hoped that the Elders might forget about me! I had never been that popular so I had high hopes that this would work!

My plan to not leave but instead take a sabbatical was a pretty good one and for the most part I was forgotten and ignored, of course I was again

"Marked" as a bad associate. I was shunned by most people, but this was fine with me and meant that I could (at that time) still see my parents whenever I wanted to. Every time I went to their house I did my best to drop little "Truth Bombs". These were facts about the Witnesses that would annoy my mum and hopefully make her think. To be honest, she hated this and frequently fell out with me but since I could now run away to my own home I was able to leave things to settle for a few days and start all over again!

During this time I still had affection for my old friends in the Kingdom Hall. I felt a sense of family. I still do feel that way with any Witness I meet, even if it's not returned. I can explain the hatred they now feel towards me very easily with one short story.

About a year after I stopped attending the meetings I was driving down the road in the pouring rain, it wasn't just raining, it was biblical rain, thunder, lightning, small children were plucked from parents arms and they watched in horror as they disappeared into the heavens, you get the picture.

It was in this storm that I saw Ted walking home. Ted was an elderly Witness, he was well into his 70's when I knew him and to be honest, he was not the most pleasant man I've ever met. His lack of charm may have been due to the fact that he had spent years of his life in a Canadian jail. Jehovah's Witnesses are accustomed to strangers moving into their Halls, men with mysterious back stories. You might hope that the story involves them serving Jehovah in distant lands and that they have amazing tales of courage and faith, perhaps even suffering imprisonment because they "Served God rather than men". Well, they often served some time in prison but it was rarely for their faith! Ted was no different as he had been in prison because he was a paedophile. After serving time for his crimes, he was then kicked out of Canada and sent back to Northern Ireland, a country he hardly knew. Now here he was about to be dissolved by sheer weight of rainwater.

Dammit though, he was a HUMAN and he was a Witness so I felt some feeling of responsibility for him. He was an old man and my parents had not raised me to allow an old man to walk miles in the pouring rain, I would have felt guilty. So, with heavy heart, I pulled over and let Ted in. He got in my car, smiled and for the first time I'd ever seen, he looked so happy.

"Thank you Steven" he kept repeating "Thank you Steven".

I was puzzled at first and wondered if Ted was going senile but then I understood. Ted had mixed me up with my brother Steven, who is slightly uglier than me but he tries! At this point, Steven had not quite been officially condemned by the Elders and so Ted was allowed to talk to him, me on the other hand....

I smiled at Ted as my car picked up speed and I started the drive to his house "Ted" I said, "you're, mistaking me for my brother Steven, I'm Neil".

Ted's smile evaporated and he looked disgusted and angry. He sat silent for a few seconds "stop the car" he said icily. "Let me out".

I nervously pulled over, only 300 metres or so closer to his home and Ted got out of my car, slammed the door behind him and never looked back as he walked on in the rain. Ted was a convicted child molester, an elderly man, yet he felt dirty by just sitting in my car. To Jehovah's Witnesses there is nothing worse than someone who leaves their cult, even a convicted child abuser.

Being a bad associate isn't all bad to be honest, they don't completely ignore you. If, they get the chance, the Witnesses will still use you to make themselves look better. As someone who had left and entered the "world" I was supposedly as bad as one could be, so it must have come as a surprise when both my and my brothers face appeared on the front page of the local newspaper under the headline "Fire Rescue Hero's".

Steven and I had been hanging out together one Thursday evening when we heard someone banging loudly at his front door. Steven and I lived in a pretty sketchy area, so we opened it slowly not sure what to expect. "Hello" said a drunk man. "The apartment across the street is on fire and I can't get them out".

We put on our shoes and told him to take us to the 3 storey building. When we got their, it was dark and everything looked normal but as soon as we touched the front door of the ground floor apartment we knew there was a real problem. The door was to hot to touch and when we opened the letter box thick black smoke poured out.

I told the man to go back to our house and call the fire brigade. Steven and I ran at the door trying to smash through it but it held. Finally, after we had resorted to kicking it in, we were able to get inside. The smoke was so thick that we had to crawl on our hands and knees in order to breathe but we were soon able to spot a man lying on a sofa. The only thing we saw was the reflective stripe on the side of his tracksuit but it was enough and Steven and I both grabbed a leg each and dragged the unconscious man outside. Steven gave him CPR. This was tough due to his huge bushy beard and the stink of booze but Steven is a trooper and while I left him to make out with his new friend, I ran back inside to look for more people.

As the fire engine pulled up outside the burning home, the windows blew out out with a bang and the firemen started putting up ladders to evacuate the people who lived upstairs. Both of us needed oxygen afterwards and the Regional Fire Commander recommended us for a Bravery Award, well actually a bravery letter, in which he made it quite clear that we should never do this again but we were indeed, very brave (and now we had a letter to prove it!).

I learned later that when it came up at the meetings that two "bad associates" had saved a man's life and been commended for it, the response was "Well they were raised in the Truth you know, some of it must have stuck". I felt like screaming "It was Thursday night you idiots! If I'd still been I Witness I'd have been at the meeting" but they wouldn't care and of course they would never listen to a bad associate anyway. I wouldn't recommend running, walking or crawling into a burning building but I can tell you for a certainty that neither my brother or I did it because we thought Jehovah was watching.

I discovered that my time inside a cult had left me both socially awkward and pretty immature, not to mention ignorant of History, Science, Art, Politics and general chit chat! I never noticed until I was out that my social skills were basically non existent and were limited to dumbly nodding my head as I waited for people to stop speaking and then throwing in a leading question like "Isn't that mass killing recently terrible?". When they'd nod a confused yes, I'd then start my cult sales pitch and instantly ruin any chance of a friendship! It's hardly surprising that I found it hard to make meaningful relationships!

One relationship that I didn't need to make was with my sister, that relationship was just waiting to restart! Since I had stopped going to the meetings, I decided to contact Karen who was going through some very serious marriage difficulties. I could think of no reason not to help her now, so I asked her to come and live with me. Karen was nervous but agreed and so one sunny day I arrived at her house with my dad and some friends and began moving her and her four children. All was going well until Karen's husband turned up and told us we couldn't have anything. This did not sit well with me, so I picked him up and carried him out of the house head first! This was the best option as my dad was charging at him with a crowbar! A month or two later I ended up paying out hundreds of pounds and receiving a court order to stay away from Karen's husband, an Order which I was happy to obey.

Having Karen and her kids in my life was wonderful. We talked about the past and cried, I said sorry and I have been able to be with her ever since, watching her children grow up to have children of their own. I have almost made up for the years of losing her but though time might heal all wounds it certainly leaves a hell of a scar.

Life After Leaving

I decided now was a great time to to find love but I had absolutely no idea how to find it. I did what I thought was the most logical thing I could, I joined an online dating agency! This was a purely wholesome one mind you, not for me the heady world of "swiping right" and instant "hook ups! Swiping right hadn't even been invented yet and I honestly wouldn't have known what to do if I had been asked to "hookup" anyway! This internet site just asked you to post some details about yourself and then let you look through, read about and possibly send a message to the lady you liked.

I was lucky, I had just started a relationship with a lovely woman called Lynda (now my wonderful wife) and it was (and is) brilliant. I still remember our first date and how strange it felt to be meeting a "Worldly" girl for a meal! When the night was over I walked her to her car and we both stood nervously waiting for the other one to make a move. I was hardly an experienced dater so I instantly came up with a plan and went with it. I looked at her and in my best Clark Gable voice said, "I'm going to kiss you now. I'm going to kiss you long and hard, like you've never bee...." Lynda laughed so hard and so long and then grabbed me by the head and kissed me and that initial joke is a pretty good example of why we have stayed married.

At first Lynda knew nothing about my old beliefs. All she knew was that it was sad that I had never had a Christmas present or a birthday party and she quickly set out to remedy these problems! She secretly arranged for me to have my first ever birthday party at the age of 30! My parents even came too as they were beginning to have more and more doubts, the feeling of having my family sing "Happy Birthday to Neil" was amazing! At first her mother warned her off, saying that I was secretly looking to get her to join the Witnesses, as if my charms would ever convince anyone to join a cult for my benefit! Nothing could be further from the truth of course and in no time at all I was composing my "Disassociation Letter" from the Jehovah's Witnesses.

Around about this time I met up with two Jehovah's Witness Elders by chance, one of them was the now quite elderly Moses from chapter 1. The men were talking about a recent Television documentary that had dealt with the subject of child sexual abuse among Witnesses and the cults refusal to deal with the problem. One of the main people interviewed was a former young Witness woman who now had several large tattoos on her face. I remember Moses speaking in his booking voice, "Well some Witness she must have been with her face all covered in tattoos!" I was working at the time but couldn't stop myself speaking up and saying, "Well if you had been raped by your father for decades and the Elders covered it up I imagine you'd be a little screwed up too".

He had nothing else to say and that was the last I ever saw of Moses. Years later I learned that he had been caught red handed breaking in to my local hospitals blood supply! He claimed that as a member of the Jehovah's Witnesses Hospital Liaison Committee committee he was "Entitled to inspect the blood". I think this descent into madness is a good place to end the story of a nasty man who wasted his life.

Leaving a cult always seems to be a pain. If you want to stop being a Catholic you just stop going to Mass. If you want to stop being a member of the Church Of England you just stop, it's really that simple.

However, if you want to stop being a Jehovah's Witness, there are certain hoops to jump through, though when you make it absolutely clear that you think it's nonsense some of those are waved!

The Witnesses are supposed to make every effort to keep you inside their cult walls but as many will tell you, this is only theoretically what they do. The reality is that your local loving Elders will try to figure out very quickly whether or not they can get you back on the plantation and keep you in line once there. If the answer is no, they will either disfellowship you or demand that you write a letter of disassociation. Often, Jehovah's Witnesses with many decades of loyal service will be spoken to once and for only a few minutes and then kicked out. This is the kind of love that Jehovah's Witnesses show behind doors while the world can't see them.

While the two options have two different names, in reality both choices amount to little more then "Did you jump or were you pushed?". Whatever path you go down, the destination is the same, Shun-town! In short order, this news will be reported to your local congregation and all it's members will know what to do, shun you as if you had died. Mothers will shun their children, husbands will shun wives and kids will shun their parents. As I told you before, I loyally ignored my own sister for well over a decade up to this point and now it was my turn! For the record I'm sure my actions could have given any number of reasons to be pushed but on this occasion I decided to jump.

Writing my letter took a few days. I had so much to say but I didn't want to overload the reader with dry information. I could have written a few words "I quit" is actually more than enough. I could have ignored the demand to write a letter completely and the Elders would simply report that they "Deemed that I was no longer a member of the Jehovah's Witnesses" allowing them to carry on to the final part of their job, but I wanted to do more. I wanted to leave with a measure of pride, so this is what I wrote.

The Governing Body of Jehovah's Witnesses

Brooklyn New York

United States of America

Dear Sirs,

I am writing for the first and last time as a member of the Jehovah's Witness religion. I was raised in this faith and was baptized at the age of twelve in the congregation in Lisburn. I remained a part of that congregation until about 1999/2000 when I stopped going, mainly because of the cruel treatment I received from several Elders.

During the last few years I have had no visits from the shepherds of my Hall. No one has tried to encourage me back into association with Jehovah's one religion. During that time I looked into your religion very deeply, and as I am sure you will know, found you lacking. I discovered the broken promises, the half-truths and lies you have told for one hundred years. I learned the things you try so desperately to hide from the Witnesses, to many to go into in this letter.

I have learned that many Elders know these things. My circuit overseer has said on the platform "There are many things I don't believe, but I still teach them". All my local Elders know the things mentioned in the various publications outlining the wrong teachings and wrong practices of your religion, but they continue to persist in this great lie.

What hurts the most is not your lies, but the results those lies have had on so many millions of people. I think of the parents who refused to inoculate their children because you said they were filthy animal puss? I think about the men and women left with no provision for old age and no children to provide for them because of your emphasis on "The end of this system of things" and "Not wanting to bring children into this sick old system" finally I think of the people who have died because of your wrong policy on blood transfusions, my own sister nearly being one of your victims.

I have seen so many good people in your religion, however I have seen cruel and evil ones too. Your claim to be uniquely clean is as false as the worship you offer to our God. I won't go into the things I or my family have suffered because of your teachings but before I end my letter I wanted to say a few things.

You were not picked out in 1914 to oversee all Gods possessions on earth. **God does not choose you.** God does not deal with selfish arrogant men who hide in ivory towers while ordering good people to live under burdens they will not touch.

You are not protecting Jehovah's name by hiding the abusers of children in your church. By doing this you only insult him and allow abuses to continue for longer.

You are not helping men become Christians by making them get out on the service once a week. While ignoring the old and sick. My own Presiding Overseer (a man in his late seventies) once said "I don't like visiting the elderly". An old women in my Hall was so long ignored in her home, she asked the sisters who eventually saw her "have I been Disfellowshipped?".

You are a wonderful example of straining the gnat while swallowing the camel. You worry about the colour of shirts Brothers wear on the platform or whether they should have a beard or not, but you ignore the most important things in a Christian life namely love of fellow man and not judging him. You have spent so long telling the world how evil Christendom is, but they would shudder at things you do everyday. And while I know of the despicable acts of some church's, I also know that they understand the concept of asking for forgiveness. You have never said sorry for your sins, you have only blamed others.

I continue to hold warm feelings for many men and women in my Hall and I am aware of the consequences of my actions, but I cannot be associated with this thoroughly unchristian group any longer.

Please make known this to my local congregation as soon as possible.

Neil Gardner

Lynda also encouraged me to take up martial arts, which I did with real enthusiasm. I started training in Mixed Martial Arts and eventually won a bronze medal in the Irish Amateur MMA Championship at light heavyweight despite being only five feet seven inches tall, I was always to lazy to cut weight!

This training was especially useful one evening when Lynda saw a man beating up his girlfriend outside my house. At her urging, I ran out to stop him and he pulled out a knife and began trying to stab me! I used my mighty MMA Push Kicks while screaming "Call the Police". His girlfriend got up, stood between us and was promptly stabbed. Lynda knelt down beside her as we waited for the police and I continued kicking the man until he gave up and his wallet fell on the ground as he ran away. When the police showed up, the first officer ran through a hedge to get to us and all I could do was hug him! Once the policeman scraped me off him, I gave him the wallet and Lynda and I went to bed. The young woman was fine and our attacker earned two and a half years in prison. I still wonder what would have happened if the old Neil had been there that night? The Neil that was nervous and weak and scared of his own shadow, probably best I never found out.

My parents had stayed loyal Witnesses for some time after I left but it became more and more difficult for them to do this. For one reason, my sister returning to our life had made my parents see the light about shunning and they made a promise to never abandon her again. The final straw for them was my regular visits to see them and the regular arguments that ensued! As I said, I would leave what I liked to call a "Truth Bomb" every time I visited and then I'd run out and wait a few days until the dust had settled only to do it all over again!

Lynda and I had booked a holiday together in Spain and before we left, I had one conversation with my mother where I brought up the fact that in the past Jehovah's Witnesses didn't bother getting married. She denied this and I offered (as I always did) to lend her *"Crisis Of Conscience"*. She took it this time and off Lynda and I flew to Majorca. Throughout our holiday, my mum phoned me and talked endlessly about what she was learning, she was finally learning the truth about the Truth! When we returned my parents had completely destroyed all their books in case the garbage men found them and became Witnesses. They were now confirmed Apostates!

Our bad luck with knives kept up on our Honeymoon in Africa. We decided to be "Adventurous" tourists and got a taxi into Mombasa's main market. While there, we were greeted by a welcoming gang of large toothy men with machetes who were determined to rob us. Our taxi driver led us into a spice shop owned by a Muslim man and his sons who stood in front of his store, also armed with machetes and threatened to kill our robbers! As they argued I stood in front of Lynda and thought "I am going to die. There is literally nothing I can do to save us".

As luck would have it, the storekeeper did it for me and we managed to escape through a back door and back to our taxi, never to leave our hotel again! If a missionary was telling me these stories from the Assembly platform I'd by spellbound but with all the negative news from around the world these day I try to remember that Muslim man and his teenage sons standing in front of us and saving our lives.

I tried to forget my past and got busy with living, as you know, I got married. I even tried out a few different brands of churches! Lynda had been raised a Presbyterian and I began attending her local church and even took part in a course called "Christianity Explored" with her. I have to be honest and say that associating with people who called themselves "Born Again" was very unnerving! I had been raised to think very poorly of anyone who was in another religion and thought that born again Christians were the epitome of bad association. So, it was a surprise to me that they were actually pretty nice folks! Lynda's church actually funded the running of an entire hospital in Uganda. They sent members over to work as administrators and paid for local kids to come over and train as nurses. When I compared this to the total and absolute absence of charitable works in my own religion I felt shamed!

About a year attending Lynda's church and endless debates and discussions with her Minister, I felt comfortable enough to get baptized, but I was not alone, my parents also got baptized in a local church which they still attend to this day! You could say that we truly washed away the sins of our old cult life that day.

After that I'm ashamed to say that I pretty much stopped having anything to do with the Jehovah's Witnesses, or Ex Jehovah's Witnesses. As I said, I got married, had children, bought a bigger house and built a better business. Truth be told, if life had continued as I'd hoped I doubt you'd ever have heard my name, but it didn't go as I'd hoped. It went from bad to worse. As 2008 rolled around and the economies of the world all took a collective nosedive my business went along with them. I lost nearly all my clients and in short order was forced to put our home up for sale.

At around the same time we discovered that Lynda had developed Cancer and she would require several major operations followed by radiation therapy, then a lifetime of medication. We even took our children to a special class to prepare them for the potential of losing their mum. Thankfully this never happened as I'd make a terrible single parent! I did learn some things during that time though.

1. There is no such thing as "A good kind of Cancer" despite what a doctor tells you.
2. Not many people will get their full health back after cancer, you just figure out how to carry on anyway.

3. Cancer is always in the back of your mind.

I think it's safe to say I wasn't in best of places at this time but it was at this point in my life that I applied to become a Prison Officer. Working in prisons in Northern Ireland is a very dangerous proposition. You aren't safe at work and you aren't safe at home. You need to check under your car for booby traps and you carry a gun to fend of assassination attempts, in fact during my service , two officers were assassinated.

Now, I'm an emotional sort and doubt I'd have thrived in the atmosphere of a prison at any time in my life but this was a terrible time and I quickly began to realize that I was so far out of my depth that I was about to drown. I remember one day when I was off work, walking my daughter to the park a car drove past us slowly, inside was a local paramilitary thug and a few members of his gang. I remember moving Emily behind me and slowly reaching for the Walther PP I carried in a hidden holster on my waist. The car slowed and they looked at me, all I though was "Please don't make me shoot you in front of my daughter". It was a very bad time.

Later the same gang threatened my life and my family spent a week with a squad of police officers armed with automatic rifles living in our back garden in case they carried out their threats.

One another occasion, while on duty I took an inmate to hospital, he had set himself on fire. As I waited for him to arrive at the front gate, two officers were led out with serious burns to their hands, they had tried to put out the flames with their hands and were much the worse for the attempt. I jumped into the ambulance and saw the prisoner, his injuries were massive and he was in severe shock but he could still speak and it was what he said that shocked me.

"How are you doing son?" he asked, this career criminal knew me. He understood how unsuited I was to working in a prison and despite his injuries was worried about ME!

"I'm OK" I replied.

"Just do your time lad" he said smiling at me through the facial burn mask the nurse had applied.

"I can't do it" I replied.

"Then you need to leave son" he said. I held that man's hand right up to the minute the ER doctors put him into an induced coma, I don't think he survived his injuries but to the end, all he cared about was me and how I was doing. I'll never forget that.

My ill conceived career in law enforcement came to a screeching halt soon after that when I went to work one Saturday and I was sent to work in a wing where the prisoners were known to be troublesome. They had been up the night before on drugs and when we went in they were angry and violent. Already 2 had sneaked away to try to strangle a prisoner with a phone cable and one told me that as soon as his door was opened he was going to kill an officer.

This resulted in us having "Limited Movement" which means only a few prisoners at a time are allowed to leave their cells. Unfortunately, this meant we were even busier as instead of calling for inmates we had to go get them. Instead of them getting their own meals we had to serve them at the door. It was during lunch that it happened. I opened a door to a prisoner and he began to walk past me to get water. I told him he couldn't leave his cell and that I'd get water for him. He smiled at me and said "Aye right", then grabbed me and pulled me into his cell. I did my best to fight back as I quite enjoy fighting, but I was 40 years old and he was 20, as was his cellmate. After a while all I remember was the prisoners across the aisle screaming "Kill him. Kill the fucking screw" (slang for officer) "Jump on his fucking head!"

I remember shouting to other officers who came swiftly. Together, we dragged the man out of his cell but by then I was finished. I think if the prisoner and I tallied up our injuries we came out even but he had grown up in a life of violence whereas I had grown up telling people about Jehovah's Kingdom! I left work early that day with the intention to return on my next shift but soon realized it wasn't going to happen. I saw councillors and developed an impressive number of stress related symptoms.

At one point I remember sitting in the house on my own thinking "If I don't do something productive I'll just shoot myself" and that's when I began to think again about my experiences as a Jehovah's Witnesses and whether any of it still affecting me.

I decided to watch YouTube videos by EX JW's. The first was JW Struggle, then Mike and Kim. Then I decided to try and tell my story. I sat one morning and made a shaky and nervous video about my years inside the cult and then put it on YouTube. Another website spread the word and I got hundreds of messages from EX JW's who had the same or worse story to tell. I made another video and another and another. In time I called my channel The Great Apostate!

Soon I had done radio interviews and Podcasts! I was getting messages every day from people around the world asking advice or support. Some needed help to find housing after their families had kicked them out, others needed a little money to get by and because I had developed a good name in the community, people trusted me to help. Today, I am still able to help people whenever I can. I have a Patreon account which I use for this.

I remember one holiday my family had in London. I was contacted on the first day by an incredibly angry young man who complained that I was insulting his religion and I was!

I decided early on that I would try to shake Witnesses out of their self induced coma by making fun of everything they hold dear. My hope was that by doing so they would feel obliged to try to defend themselves and this would give me a chance to talk frankly to them, it works every time.

This young man raged at me for a full week but like a big shark I reeled him in slowly. The only down side was that I saw nothing of London! Every time Lynda turned around I was emailing this guy. In the end, we stopped speaking and I wondered if it had been worthwhile at all, until six months later when I got another email from him.

Dear Neil

You might not remember but we talked a few months ago. I wanted to thank you for taking the time to help me think through what I believed and telling me about the JW's. It's thanks to people like you that I'm writing this from the departure lounge of my local airport and am about to fly across the country to go to University. I've left the Jehovah's Witnesses and I'm never going back.

People look at EX JW activists and might think "All they do is make ten minute videos. How hard is that?" Well they're right, that's the easy part. The hard part is the evenings spend late into the night talking to hurt, angry and damaged people. Days spent reading death threats and suicide letters from people who are in such pain they feel they can't go on.

I have had to deal with that many times and spent one memorable day on the phone to 3 different American State Police forces trying to get them to go visit a lonely EX JW who messaged me "Ending it now. No pain any more". Making videos is usually easy, caring for broken people is 24/7.

Thankfully I'm not alone, I'm not even the biggest part of a global network of EX JW activists who are here to help each other. When I look at what others have done I feel so inadequate. I know of men who have gone to prison because they won't stop speaking out against child sex abuse in the Jehovah's Witnesses. I know others who have spent small fortunes fighting this cult and still others who have literally no spare time due to the commitments they have taken on, compared to them I'm a part-timer.

I actually took the time to count how many hours my videos had been watched by people all over the world and was amazed! I realized that If I had still been a Regular Pioneer in the Jehovah's Witnesses and spending the required (in my day) 90 hours a month going from door to door I would need to live for nearly 300 years to come close to matching what I have managed to do. It seems I am a much better "Apostate Pioneer" than I ever was an actual Pioneer!

I actually mentioned this once in one of my videos and was immediately met with the reply, "It's easy to see you were once a Jehovah's Witness Neil. You're still counting your time!" You can take the man out of the Kingdom Hall but not the Kingdom Hall out of the man!

Unshunning For Fun

I have been shunned and ignored by almost every single person I have ever known. All the people I called "Brother" and "Sister", all the people that as a child you called "Uncle" and "Auntie" even though they weren't even related but our families were simply so close. Being shunned is not usually much fun, it's embarrassing and cruel and makes you look and feel like a dick in public, unless you don't let yourself be shunned.

Most former Jehovah's Witnesses have no idea that, like the tango, shunning takes two! It turns out that it is incredibly difficult to not talk to someone if they keep talking to you, so that's exactly what I decided to do. I made the decision to not be shunned. I decided that whenever I saw an old friend who now thought that I was to terrible to speak to I would do all the speaking for them! I have walked up to former friends as they sat in doctor's offices or stood beside those tacky little information carts they have nowadays but the most fun I've had with with shunning was one day in the local supermarket.

I was shopping for groceries with my wife and walking slowly through the meat section when I saw and old Witness friend and his wife, we were walking towards each other and I knew that they knew I was there. They started looking frantically around and then became intensely interested in some products on the bottom shelf. I walked up to them.

"Hi David, Hi Mary, whatcha doing down there" I asked cheerfully.

"Umm, Hello Neil" David replied, at this point Mary was literally dragging him away but if one thing in life is true it is this, when you see someone you know in a supermarket you will see them again and again in every aisle!

We met again at beside the baked beans, "So how's it going" I said with a smile on my face. "Ahhhhh, not bad Neil, How are you" David said while Mary gave me a half smile but then they walked away quickly.

"Ohh I'm doing great" I said as we both reached for milk a few minutes later, "Lot's of free time these days".

It soon became obvious to them that shunning is a two way street and in a supermarket all streets lead to me and my constant chatter! I have actually heard stories of exJW's being visited by Elders who were there to tell them off for not honouring the shunning rules! Needless to say my local Elders never bothered to visit me but now they do walk away a little faster if they see me coming!

So What Now?

This book is about my experience as a Jehovah's Witness. It's also about why I left and what I did afterwards. I sincerely hope that it amused you and made you laugh out loud in places. If that's all you came for, thanks for reading it's been fun! I hoped to enjoyed the bit about my bunker building disasters and my love affair with our ancient woodlands. This book was also written for people like me, people who left, suddenly on the outside, alone, afraid and searching. It's to them I'll be writing to now but stay tuned all you folks with your shit together because we'll all finish up together at the end!

Good question Neil! So What now? What do you do after a lifetime spent inside a controlling and all encompassing cult? What will you believe? Where will you go? Which church will you attend? Will you get involved in the world around you? What about politics? These and many other questions have been asked by me and a lot of other people, some have even asked me!

Anyone who has spent their lives being told what to think and say about almost every subject, will feel more than a little confused when they first step outside into the world and realise that not only was what they believed for so long totally wrong. There isn't another system that they can jump into right away. Well, there are systems waiting to accept former cult members, they're called cults! It's not unusual to see an ex Jehovah's Witness leave and become a Mormon, or a Mormon leave their church and join the Jehovah's Witnesses! If you have never been taught to think for yourself the prospect of being forced to do so later in life can seem impossible. Better to let someone else think for you.

I want to be careful, at this point, to warn the reader that they not take my words as doctrine either. I am in many ways a very disappointing Messiah! and I don't advise anyone follow me to closely! Instead of following me or anyone else I think it's possible, admirable even, to take certain ideas and use them to follow your own path. In a sense, we are all living in a kingdom of the blind but with some thought and effort on our part we can equip ourselves with a stick and maybe even recover a little vision too! So if you will bare with me for a few minutes and let me tell you what I think about this most important of subjects.

The ex cult member is often left seeking something for the rest of their lives, you might call it truth or a purpose, but when I left I wanted to find the "Real truth". I thought I'd found it through deep study of the Bible and came to the decision that it could be summed in the words "Sola Scriptura" or "By the Bible Alone". I reasoned that all the faults I had seen so far in my life were due to an incorrect understanding and interpretation of the Bible and like the Christians of old, I could simply rely solely and completely on the words written inside the Holy Scriptures.

I'd love for this to be true but I discovered that, as much as I wanted the Bible to be my lodestone in life, it was often lacking when I needed it. Like anyone else who studied the Bible I was left with doubts with some of the things I read. Histories that disgusted me and teachings I felt were at best just OK. The problem with "Sola Scriptura" is that the Bible alone has some terrible stuff in it and I don't feel inclined to support it's message.

Was it alright when Jehovah made poisonous snakes enter the camp of the wandering Israelites in order to bite them all because they bitched about the boring diet? What about getting them to make a giant copper serpent to get better and isn't that exactly what he killed them for in the past, making a graven image? My kids bitch about eating pasta all the time and I have never send a poisonousness snake to kill them, just regular snakes!

Do I really need to praise God because he ordered a bear to kill a gang of brats who called the prophet Elisha a "Bald head"? Sure, as a bald man, I feel a certain brotherly sympathy for Elisha and I too have tasted the salty stigma and shame of hearing kids make fun of my shiny head. I'm not certain watching my children being torn limb from limb and then devoured by a grizzly bear would make me happy. Call me crazy, but I'm a people person!

I remember reading the story of Job as a child and learning the message in it, something about not being cheeky to god, even if he kills your family. Even though I was very young I remember feeling pretty pissed off on behalf of Job's family! Sure, it's not great to get boils but I think the real victims in this twisted morality play are his kids and I'm not at all certain that letting a house fall on them was the best way to test Job's character.

"But you mustn't blame God Neil" I hear you say. OK why?

"Because God cannot be blamed for anything bad and only does good". Who said?

"Ummm, he did!".

Well that's pretty convenient! In the future, when my kids come to me and rightfully complain about all times I was a shitty father, I'll whip this piece of circular logic out of my pocket and smile like I just won the argument. Or like Jehovah, maybe I'll shout down on them thunderously and say "Who are you to criticise me? You try walking in my shoes and tell me how much better you'd be". Yeah, I'm definitely doing that one.

It wasn't the Bibles words that made me quit being a Christian, it was my own experience that did me in. In particular, it was our first child who was never born. We called him Gor which was short for Grain of Rice, because that's how big he was when we lost him. It was my wife's miscarriage that made me rethink my belief in a God, who could allow anyone to experience the pain we felt that day. If you've gone through this too (I'm really sorry) you'll know what I mean when I tell you, that it's a pain so intense that you feel that you could stab yourself and not notice the extra sensation.

It wasn't the fact that we lost a baby that made me doubt God, but the fact that I had been blindly going to church and smiling, singing my heart out while all the while others were screaming out in misery and pain as I now was. How fucking selfish I had been to believe in a God who loves me, while ignoring the suffering all around me because my life was going well. "If God can't make pain go away then what use was he?" I thought.

Not long after losing our first child I stopped going to church or praying and I made a decision to try to find a way to live that was consistent with my values but would also be one I could defend in a room full of suffering people. Surprisingly, I was not alone in my search!

For as long as men and women could think, they have asked the same questions, "Why are we hear?" "How did we get here?" "What's the meaning of life?". There are lots more but let's just stick with these ones today, you can try answer the rest tomorrow. As I said earlier, the problem many people face is that asking hard questions is hard! It's far easier listen to others ask those questions rhetorically and then listen to their answers.

People have missed the fact, that this solution to life's problems has directly led to Nazi Germany, Communist Russia, Maoist China and hundreds of inspiring posters like "Keep Calm and Carry On" or the one with the kitten balancing on a rope with the words "Hang In There Baby" above it. Basically, taking other peoples advice is not always a great idea, so what do you do?

Wisdom is the application of knowledge, learned through our own suffering and mistakes. You're going to make mistakes and suffer anyway so the least you can do is get a little wisdom out of the experience! The greatest lovers of wisdom in history were the ancient Greeks, they loved wisdom so much they invented a whole new way of thinking and called it "Philosophy" which means love of wisdom. That is what I want to tell you about today.

Everyone has heard the word philosophy. The extent they know about the subject might be limited to quasi intellectual questions about trees falling down in empty forests and what sound they make and if that's your limit I understand. Philosophy isn't taught much at all and when it is, it's often made to be dull and wordy but in reality Philosophy is simply a system that allows it's users to make decisions about their lives based on clear principles.

It gives them tools to hear others impartially and judge accurately if what they said was truth or bullshit. It allows parents to teach their kids useful truths without filtering them through stories where bears eat kids or they get bitten to death by snakes for complaining about lacklustre menu options. Finally, it gives you the chance to build a workable replacement for the faulty system that ex-cult members once followed. If philosophy accomplished just one of the things I've mentioned, it would be reason enough to learn more, if it manages to achieves all four it'd be a miracle!

Don't be put off by the word philosophy. We all lived by a philosophy once, it was just a really bad one! One of the core principles in my former philosophy was "Don't bring disrepute on Jehovah's name". That was wheeled out by Jehovah's Witness leadership whenever you were cheated, robbed or a child was raped to stop the victim or their parents from going to the police. Jehovah's Witnesses would be made to look bad if the public knew that members were just as evil and dishonest if not more so than the rest of society so you'd best keep your mouth shut! Wouldn't it be nice if the philosophy you followed wasn't a cause for guilt and self loathing? This will by no means be a thorough discussion of philosophy but I would like to tell you about a few of the things I have come to love and that I try to teach my own kids.

1. Think for yourself but first learn how to think.

I was once fooled so completely and totally that I thought that I was part of God's elect on earth and that one day soon I'd be saved while billions of others would die. That sounds pretty ridiculous in hindsight and would have seemed silly then if I had just thought for myself. Thinking for yourself is great but it won't help if you don't know how to think in the first place.

Use your gut. If something feels wrong, it probably is. If the idea of God killing seven billion people but leaving the paedophile in your church alive sounds wrong? that's because it is wrong.

Learn Critical Thinking skills. Don't base your views on assumptions and challenge ones you have. If you aren't allowed to read books critical of the church you belong to it's probably because your church gave up trying to refute those criticisms a long time ago.

Go where the truth leads you and don't be put off. Though be pragmatic, you have spent enough time being a martyr for "The Truth", maybe you should take it easy for a while.

Read and learn from others who have seen more and know more than you do. Take their wisdom and try to make it your own, you'll fail more often than you succeed but it's worth the effort.

2. Be unwavering in standing up for truth.

It's easy to go back on what you know to be true once you get pressed to by others, try not to. You don't need to die fighting for what you believe, but I think we lose a little piece of what makes us decent people whenever we back away from what's true.

When Galileo was dragged before the Pope to apologise for saying that the Earth revolved around the Sun, he's rumoured to have whispered on his knees "Yet it moves" sometimes all we can do is whisper "Yet it moves" and sometimes that's enough.

3. Understand how you were fooled and don't let it happen again.

Once you understand how dishonest people win arguments, you'll become a much harder target in life. Learn the tricks they use to win arguments for starters!

Appeal to Authority- These fallacies occur when someone accepts a truth on blind faith just because someone they admire said it.

Katherine loves Tom Cruise. One day, she meets Tom Cruise and he tells her unicorns live in New York City. Without searching to find out if fairy tales have sprung to life in the mid-town Manhattan, she believes it to be true.

Princess Kate wears Alexander McQueen. Are you trying to say you have better fashion sense than a royal princess?

Appeal to Ignorance- These fallacies occur when someone asserts a claim that must be accepted because no one else can prove otherwise.

People have been praying to God for years. No one can prove h doesn't exist. Therefore, he exists.

Since the students have no questions concerning the topics discussed in class, the students are ready for a test.

Appeal to Pity- These fallacies occur when someone seeks to gain acceptance by pointing out an unfortunate consequence that befalls them.

"Don't leave the Jehovah's Witnesses, it would crush your mother".

Begging the Question - Also called Circular Reasoning. This type of fallacy occurs when the conclusion of an argument is assumed in the phrasing of the question itself.

If God didn't make the earth, who did?

The leadership of the Jehovah's Witnesses is the Faithful and Discreet Slave spoken of in the Bible because we say so and you should believe that because we are the Faithful and Discreet Slave spoken of in the Bible.

False Dilemma - These fallacies occur when someone is only given two choices for possible alternatives when more than two exist.

You're either with us or against us, there's no in between.

Red Herring - These fallacies occur when someone uses irrelevant information to distract from the argument.

"They Left the Jehovah's Witnesses and now they're celebrating Christmas!" when discussing people who sincerely disagree with their former cults teachings.

Slippery Slope - These fallacies occur when someone assumes a very small action will lead to extreme outcomes.

If we celebrated birthdays pretty soon we'd be worshipping Satan!

Straw Man Fallacy - These fallacies occur when someone appears to be refuting the original point made, but is actually arguing a point that wasn't initially made.

"Our founder Charles Taze Russell never said he was a prophet" when denying accusations that he claimed to be so. That's true, he allowed it to be printed in his own magazine and allowed members to call him a prophet, but he never said so himself.

Sweeping Generalizations- These fallacies occur when a very broad application is applied to a single premise.

Watchtower 1995 Mar 15 p.1

"The majority of people have no interest in God and his purposes."

Ad Hominem (Attacking the Person)- These fallacies occur when an acceptance or rejection of a concept is rejected based on its source, not its merit.

Watchtower 2011 July 15

"Apostates are 'mentally diseased', and they seek to infect others with their disloyal teachings."

Band Wagon - These fallacies occur when a proposition is claimed to be true or good solely because many people believe it to be so.

Everyone at The Kingdom Hall Is getting baptized and so should you?

Everyone else believes what was in the latest magazine why are you so special?

Post Hoc, Ergo Propter Hoc - These fallacies occur when it is assumed that, because one thing happened after another, it must have occurred as a result of it.

Jehovah's Witnesses believe the Last Days commenced in 1914, supposedly evidenced by dramatic increases in sickness, famine, war, earthquakes and crime.

4. Learn to argue without cmotion

This one is my favourite! When we argue our views it's very easy to get emotional and act as if the person disagreeing with our thoughts is attacking us. This is a mistake and serves to bind us to bad ideas because we have mistaken those ideas for ourselves. You are not what you believe, often what you think today will be wrong tomorrow, and possibly right again next year.

I get my kids to practice this by getting to have various arguments with me about things they have really strong feelings about, chocolate for dinner for example! I then ask them to argue the point from the position against chocolate for dinner. They hated it at first but now enjoy thinking of reasons that their position may be right and as former cult members we were taught to accept what we were told and never argue or ponder over what we heard.

Learn to discuss any subject with good grace and without turning red when you get challenged.

5. Seek the most good

If in doubt about your actions, seek the most good to the most people. You might be wrong about any number of things but by seeking the most good to those around you it will allow you to quickly handle tough problems without wringing your hands or dithering.

6. Keep an open mind

You are just one person. You are at best, an expert in only one or two things and you are unlikely to be that much smarter than anyone else you meet. Keep an open mind when forming new opinions. Accept that if the facts change you'll change with them. Understand that you are prone to biases and petty dislikes and being wrong isn't a crime, being stubborn should be!

7. Accept your own limitations

Sad that you can't fix the world? Disappointed that you don't have all the answers? YOU ARE NOT ALONE! We all need to accept our limitations and admit that we will very likely only affect a tiny change in out lives.

Kids who join the Army will often say they want to serve a higher purpose and religious people will say the same thing. We need to get used to the fact that it's hard to do that and even if you succeed, you might be wrong. I am just a single man. I am, in many ways a huge disappointment to myself and I constantly worry about how I am seen or how my actions effect others. This message is mostly to myself. One man (or woman) can make a difference but it's really hard and we need to realistic about what we can achieve and not hold ourselves to impossible standards like we used to do.

You'll notice that nothing I just wrote told you what to think or who to follow, that's your job. I have met ex cult members who went on to become Evangelical Christians, Muslims or aggressive Atheists. I have talked with ex Jehovah's Witnesses who have become Communists and Fascists and everything in between. I have spoken to some who have become half assed Gurus and others who became Flat Earthers. What those people became was their choice and I hope they made it after careful thought, using the tools above would have ensured that they did.

An insult often thrown at ex-Jehovah's Witnesses by angry current members is that we are divided, we fight among each other that the only thing we all agree on is that we are right but this argument is only partly correct. Sure there are lots of ex-Jehovah's Witnesses I know and disagree with, lots more I know and love but whether we do or do not agree on theology, ethics, politics or our various styles of activism we do share one thing and that is that we are FREE TO MAKE OUR OWN MINDS UP.

We can each read and make our own decisions based on what we feel is best for ourselves, our families and society as a whole. We may be wrong, we may be right but we came to our opinions freely and fairly. We didn't get fake truth, served hot and steaming from the bowels of a fake religion, served up by fake friends who will throw us away like trash if we dare think for ourselves and that seems a fair bargain.

Learning some basic philosophy will help you come to conclusions that can be trusted to stand the test of time. They will give you courage and hope to walk away from false religion, or all religion if you want to and it will take away the constant fear many ex cult members have every day, "What if they're right?" If they are right (they aren't don't worry) you can answer that doubt with this reply,

"I am not perfect and have made many mistakes but I am an honest person and honestly tried to understand what I was taught to be true. It did not satisfy me or millions of others like me and I can't be a part of something I don't believe to be true. I will seek to learn more every day and make good choices using the truths I do believe in. If I'm wrong I was wrong in good faith. If there is a day of judgement I hope and trust I judged as fairly I judge others and my faults forgiven as I am only human".

If you are escaping a cult or are just out of one. If you got out years ago or if you just read this book because it sounded funny, I wish you happiness and success.

I hope you can get past your past and go on to live a wonderful life free in the knowledge that you are better than the cult you left behind and though the leaving may cause you to hurt more than you thought possible, it is worth it all, if you keep trying to make it so.

If you can't get out of your cult now because your family is still a part of it, please remember that sometimes just whispering "Yet it moves" is all we can do. Every one of us now free, once did just that because we could do nothing more. Not everyone who leaves the Jehovah's Witnesses is an Apostate, some are reluctant Apostates and a few are great Apostates.

What you choose to be is your choice, your freedom, whatever choice you make I hope it is one that makes you happy and I look forward to hearing what you do with your freedom!

Afterward

It's a cold September 2015 in Dublin. Lynda and I have taken the kids to watch an International Rugby game at Lansdowne Road between Ireland and Canada. We have front row seats and watch as the teams come out of their changing rooms and line up for the national anthems. This moment would once have brought me out in a sweat! As a young child in Canada, I remember standing for the Canadian national anthem in school but refused to put my hand over my heart because this was what Jehovah demanded of me.

Since then I had avoided uncounted occasions when I would have been expected to stand for the British national anthem and I remember at least a dozen times I was caught out and had to endure the angry stares of patriotic Brits as I stood out like a sore thumb.

Tonight is different, tonight is a first. Tonight as the band starts playing "Oh Canada" I stand beside my wife and put my hand on my heart and sing the song with a thousand others, even though we're surrounded by a sea of green jerseys supporting Ireland at home!

"Oh Canada my home and native land, true patriot love in all thy sons command"

I feel connected to a country I love like never before, connected to society and no longer a self made freak.

"With glowing hearts we see thee rise, the true north strong and free"

I am standing beside me wonderful wife, who I'd never have met if I had remained a Jehovah's Witness and we are both singing as loudly as we can.

"From far and wide oh Canada we stand on guard for thee"

I look down at my two children, neither will ever know what it's like to be in a miserable little cult that limits their lives and minds and stunts their hearts, and they're singing right along like the good little Canadians they are!

"God keep our land glorious and free. Oh Canada we stand on guard for thee. Ohhhh Canada we stand on guaaaard for theeeeeee"

Tonight is a great night. I feel connected to non Jehovah's Witnesses. It is just a small example of the hundreds of experiences I've missed out on as Jehovah's Witness (it was after all a meeting night!) one more little way that I was made an outcast but not any more. From now on I am worldly, more than that I am an Apostate but I am not just an Apostate, I am a great Apostate. I am The Great Apostate.

Postscript

There are nearly eight million Jehovah's Witnesses on the Earth as I write this paragraph, you might work with one. You probably think they are happy people, they aren't.

They carry the misery that comes with being responsible for a never ending preaching work. They carry the stress of constant time and financial pressure but that's not all, they are victims. Many of abuse, both mental and physical, and they need help to see that the cult they think loves unconditionally that only cares about its secrecy and there dollars.

In time, most Witnesses will leave their cult. They'll be damaged but they'll leave. So the next time you meet a Jehovah's Witnesses spare a thought for their plight and tell them it's OK to think for yourself, to doubt and to read. Hopefully you'll be helping them get out a little faster.

Bonus Chapter!
Warwick Protest 5th November 2017

Shortly after I finished writing this book, I was contacted by two of my EX JW friends, Joel and Parker, they had a wonderful idea and wanted me to be a part of it.

They, along with a few others planned a mass protest outside the front gates of the Jehovah's Witnesses "Fortress" Headquarters. Not just a protest though, they wanted to get media attention and meet up in Warwick, New York to do "Reverse Witnessing". They wanted to arrange this event to take place over an entire weekend, we would stay in the same or nearby hotels and meet up for meals in the evening. We would do podcasts and talk to each other, it was a grand idea.

I had heard about the big plans for November the 5th for a while but hadn't paid to much attention since I live thousands of miles away and didn't have the cash needed to come along. What I did hear sounded fun and I wished them well. So imagine my surprise when Joel and Parker contacted me to ask me to come along and join in, they even offered to help me fly over! Once I asked my wife if I could go (Yes, I'm a beaten man) I quickly said yes and made plans to go to America.

One thing I want to say about America, I LOVE America. I love everything about it and in an ideal world would live there, shooting guns and driving ludicrously oversized pickups trucks until I die of a bagel induced heart attack. This trip was different, even though I'd never been to New York before, this trip felt like a homecoming of sorts. As a youngster, I had dreamed of moving to America to work at the World

Headquarters of Jehovah's Witnesses and here I was, travelling to that very place but for very different reasons.

I flew into Stewart International Airport in the middle of the night on the 4th of November and got a rental car, which I couldn't start. When I did, I couldn't get it in gear, it was an automatic! I returned to the counter to beg for help and when I got back to my car there were four guys inside looking around it. "How kind of you to help" I said, "Do you work here?". Three of them looked at me, jumped out of the car and ran off. One guy said to me as he walked away, "Naaaaw man, I was just lookin". I got into the car, locked the doors and drove off in terror.

I got to my hotel in Malwah, New Jersey and walked inside. Before I had made it to the front desk I realized I was in the middle of an EX JW Apostate Convention! There was Gilbert Gonzalez (GG4GB) Parker (Fateful Slave) Rebecca (Spoonfednomore) just to name a few. Across the room and sitting in a small kitchen area was the phenomenon that is Zeb and the amazing Spike R. I met so many other wonderful people that weekend, Lori, Jo, Stacy and Paul, Maggie and her kids and Angie, the lady who took it upon herself to stop me driving on the wrong side of the road all weekend! Finally, Joel walked in (The Unwitness). That man is a giant! He is also a gentleman and took so much on himself that weekend!

We met, hugged and laughed all weekend. We "Unwitnessed" to everyone we saw. We ate and drank into the night and even though the trip still cost my family a fortune, it was well worth it. I met lots of EX JW's who had just come along to support us. They had never said a word about what they had endured when they were Witnesses or what had forced them to leave but they came to stand together and trade stories.

I also met a wonderful lady called Nancy one evening who hugged me tightly and started asking me "How are your children?,you wife? your dog Cinnamon?". It turned out Nancy had been watching my YouTube channel for a long time and felt like she knew me. She was so kind and had presents for my whole family and even helped me with some of the costs of getting to New York! Thank you Nancy.

We drove into Warwick en-mass and got back into the "Door to door work" only this time their was no-one to take out time sheets! We knocked on peoples homes, stood in the main street in town with banners calling attention to the various scandals of the Jehovah's Witnesses, all while being followed by a documentary film crew!

The results we got were staggering. How many times in the life of a Jehovah's Witness will they get someone honking their horn in support of their work? Zero, that's how many. We were shown such support and love around the town that I felt at home immediately. The honking and thumbs up never ended. The day before, "GG4GB" had been at a meeting with local council leaders who were no fans of cults being built in their backyard!

On the day of the main protest, a group went off early to do "Kingdom Hall Crashing", sadly I missed it as I had to pee! The Jehovah's Witnesses have open meetings so it's perfectly legal to attend one, even if you are an Apostate! Once there, one of you gets up and tells the assembled audience why you left the cult and continues talking until you are marched outside. Then another person stands up and another and another until you run out of people.

This causes massive disruption to the meeting and is possibly the only chance most Witnesses will get to see up close the consequences of the evil policies they force people to follow. As a tactic it's not without its detractors, some say it's needlessly confrontational. Others say it makes EX JW's look exactly as they are portrayed to Witnesses, as angry, bitter demon possessed crazies. For the record, I say it takes an incredibly strong character to be able to walk into a building full of the very people who now despise you and lovingly tell them that they are trapped in a lie. Furthermore, I'd say that the whole point of leaving any high control group is so that you can take that control back for yourself.

You don't need to take my opinion to heart or anyone else's. YOU decide how to protest and indeed whether you do protest or not. If you decide that invading Kingdom Hall's or District Assemblies isn't for you, I totally understand. I'm not sure how I feel about it to be honest but I do know one thing. Anyone who sees the victims of childhood sexual abuse or people who lost their entire families to shunning and tells them, "That's not how you should complain. You need to do it my way" is walking a thin line between being an idiot and being deranged.

If you are a victim of the Watchtower Society, you can do whatever you want to do to tell others. Just stay within the law and make sure whatever you are doing is not harming your mental health or future wealth, you gave away enough to this cult don't waste the rest of your life on it too.

We met for the protest at a local state park and I was very pleased to see so many people there. Alongside the media, we had about fifty EX JW's including several in disguise! When you consider that we were protesting a cult that requires people to wear a disguise to do so for fear of repercussions it was pretty amazing we got so many to attend that cold rainy day.

People came from all over America, Canada, Mexico and even Italy and Ireland! We gave several short speeches and made preparations for the drive to JW HQ. At one point the police arrived, having been warned of our potential for violence by a disgruntled critic looking to cause trouble. Three of us approached them and spent half an hour explaining why we were there, when we left they kept a police car on duty to guard our cars and both Officers had spent their time watching the videos of various EX JW You tubers!

We arrived at the front gates of JW HQ around noon and were greeted with the kind of love that Jesus talked about, they turned the sprinklers on us! Parker, who was one of the organisers walked up to the main gates to invite a representative from the Governing Body to come down to talk to us. Remember that this is supposedly a Christian religion, the ONLY True Christian religion and they follow the teachings of Jesus Christ and his father in heaven Jehovah, so they must do things properly right?

Now, it's been a while since I was a member but I distinctly remember being told that both of those fella's are never happier than when they recover a "Lost sheep" so they must have been ecstatic when so many lost sheep walked right up to the front door. So what did they do to bring us back to the flock? That's right, they called the Cops.

It turns out, that the one group of people most keen to avoid being a part of Satan's world were quite happy to use the world to help them get rid of a bunch of malcontents. It didn't matter though as we got plenty of publicity for our cause and far more importantly, we gave a lot of EX JW's the opportunity to get their feelings off their chest, all under the watchful eye of national media and secretive Jehovah's Witness film crews!

The best thing for me that day was the masses of signs that ranged all along the road but the greatest sign was hand written by one young women who came along with her mum. She had left the Witnesses as a young girl and had told me how terrified she had been to celebrate any "Worldly" holidays. As time went on, she became more comfortable with them and eventually grew to love them. I was so proud to stand beside her while she waved her sign at the sour faced security goons in their bullet proof bunker across the road! Her sign read

"You Lied

Christmas Is Awesome!"

We ended the protest a few hours later knowing that the small group at the protest had been followed worldwide by thousands more on multiple live-stream podcasts and also on Rick Fearons radio show "Six Screens Of The Watchtower". Rick has been exposing the Jehovah's Witnesses for many, many years and was an absolute gentleman. It was entirely my pleasure to be a part of his show and I hope he'll allow me on again.

On the final evening, we met up and had a group meal before doing a special "Live broadcast" of "The Vast Apostate Hour" YouTube channel. I remember telling Angie and several others that this trip had been an amazing experience for me. At times, I had felt like a rock star as people approached me to tell me how much they appreciated the work I do on my YouTube channel. They hugged me and tried to buy me a second and third meal! It was very strange for a self employed carpet cleaner from Northern Ireland!

As we walked to the restaurant laughing about the bizarre situation I'd found myself in, I squeezed past a lady who looked me in the eye and shouted "Is that you Neil?" and proceeded to hug me! After letting me go she went on to tell me that she was in touch with her children again for the first time in a decade after they had seen my videos on YouTube. She said her kids had left the Witnesses and they were a family again. She told me that I was (in part) responsible for that happening. I am 43 years old, at the time of writing this and I think it'll be hard to feel more proud than I did when I heard that.

Later on some said that a few of the organisers were "Like Elders" or "Wanted Praise". Speaking for myself, I can tell you that nothing could be farther from the truth. In fact, at one point, Joel was so uncomfortable with all the people congratulating him that I took him aside to tell him that he needed to lighten up and accept the compliments. I told him that he didn't realize how important this event was for so many of those present and they needed to tell him so. As for seeking praise or attention, I can tell you that all of us who had anything to do with that wonderful weekend have gone back to our lives. Nobody started a cult or begged for money and we all did it because we could and it needed to happen.

We ended the weekend as it began, unwitnessing to a group of Africa American Jehovah's Witnesses who were forced to share a cramped hotel dinning room with us! I got chills when Zeb spoke up to the teenage boys as they walked past us "We were like you guys, don't be fooled. Go to jwfacts.com". As they started to walk away each of us picked a different JW to speak to and the unwitnessing began!

I watched several of our women speak to two Elders outside. I think it was Lori who asked him "What would you do if it was YOUR daughter or granddaughter who was sexually abused by a paedophile in the Kingdom Hall?"

"It would just one of those things" he replied.......

Then it was time to say goodbye and go home. I honestly hated leaving, even though I missed my wife and kids. This had been the first time in so many years that I had felt completely at home with the people around me. As EX JW's we are often outcasts, wherever we go, not welcome in the Kingdom Hall and unable to interact with normal folks but this was different. I met people who had the same story as me. Brought up the same way and dealing with the same issues because of it. We shared our stories and laughed together. If I never get to experience another protest, I'll be very disappointed and I feel incredibly lucky to have been able to be there even once and I hope you can enjoy the feeling one day too.

I was asked to make a short speech at one point and have included it below as it encapsulates my feelings about the brotherhood of EX JW's around the world, I'll let that speech be my last words. Thank you for reading.

"H L Mencken, a native of Baltimore said "The desire to save men is often a false face to hide the desire to rule them"

We were all part of a group that claimed that it wanted to save mankind but in it's methods it showed and continues to show a desire to rule them. Their methods have destroyed lives, ripped families apart, put children in danger of sexual abusers and caused countless deaths through a dogged and false understanding of how blood should be used in medical emergencies.

If you or I were guilty of just one of those crimes I have no doubt that we would run to the nearest police station to turn ourselves in. If we had caused children to be harmed like the cruel men inside this dirty cult we would take our lives but that's not what the leadership of the JW's have done, instead they went a different route.

They have claimed divine authority to order members to shun victims, hide sexual criminals and turn those of us who are disgusted at what we see into outcasts. They call us apostates, as if we are the ones who abandoned god.

They call us mentally ill as if our revulsion at seeing innocent lives destroyed is abnormal. Well it's not abnormal. What is abnormal is running a dirty cult solely for your own benefit and claiming that only you and the elderly gerontocracy you are part of are qualified to preach the bible and who cares if a few million suffer or die to keep you in luxury.

It's abnormal to cover up tens of thousands of child rapists under the guise of "not bringing reproach upon Jehovah's name". When you ignore child abuse and punish victims you become a criminal and you prove once and for all that you are unfit to teach anyone anything, let alone tell others how to please god.

We came here to tell the Jehovah's witness community that they are wrong. We are here to tell them that we love them and most importantly we are here to tell them that the emperors who run their cult are naked, they have no truth, no Insight and no love for you whatsoever. We also came to warn the public about a dangerous cult that is hiding among them. A cult that claims to want to save you but in reality wants to rule over you and your family.

When they knock on your door ask yourself who is knocking? Are they a danger to your children, have they been involved in child abuse or covering up sexual abusers and I would ask people what do they say when you ask them these questions? Most will scurry away like a cockroach exposed to the sun because even though they will never admit it they know the truth.

We came here today because we are still Brothers and Sisters. Despite being called Apostates and shunned by our family and friends. We are true Brothers and Sisters because our relationships are not dependant on believing the ever changing lies a cult leader tells us. We have different opinions and values but we respect each other anyway, Jehovah's witnesses can be like that too.

Leaving a cult doesn't ruin your life it gives you a life! It allows you to fulfil your dreams and help others in ways those still trapped inside can only dream of. There is a vast army of Apostates who are here to help you escape, to free you from a century old lie that has only caused hurt. Most Jehovah's witnesses want to leave but they are afraid of what will happen, we can show them how good life is in the sunlight.

When you learn the truth about the truth you can never go back and we will help you move forward as real friends, real brothers real sisters. They want to escape, let's do what we can to help them. "

Neil Gardner, Warwick NY, November 5, 2017.

Appendix:
Places to go to learn more about the Jehovah's Witnesses

• Jwfacts.com - The best site for learning "The Truth About The Truth"

• www.jehovahs-witness.com[1]

• Where to go to meet EXJW's and discuss our shared past

◦ www.sixscreensofthewatchtower.com[2]

◦ The Reddit group "exjw", this is another popular group for EXJW's to meet up and chat

• Facebook has many groups, some better than others. I have been on most groups over time and left a few as they can be a bit authoritarian. I like *'The Vast Apostate Hour'* as I help run this group but there are hundreds to choose from.

• YouTube has lots of EXJW channels. My own is *'The Great Apostate'* but I would recommend you visit the following:

◦ Fifth

◦ JW Struggle

◦ Spoonfednomore

---

1. http://www.jehovahs-witness.com/

2. http://www.sixscreensofthewatchtower.com/

◦ Mike and Kim

◦ Susan Gaskin Fusco

◦ What's up Watchtower

◦ The Unwitness

◦ Fateful Slave

◦ I'm Worldly

◦ ExJW Critical Thinker

◦ Stacey Lopez

◦ Katy Kitten

◦ The Unreluctant

Some of the best sites are not even on this list because I don't know about them! Every day another EXJW rises up and tells their story, will you be next?

Books to read about the Jehovah's Witnesses

- *"Crisis of Conscience"* by Raymond Franz

- *"In Search Of Christian Freedom"* by Raymond Franz

- *"Sign of The Last Days When"* by Carl Olof Jonsson[3] and Wolfgang Herbst[4]

---

3. https://www.amazon.co.uk/Carl-Olof-Jonsson/e/B001KMSHX4/ref=dp_by-line_cont_book_1

- *"The Gentile Times Reconsidered"* by Carl Olof Jonsson

- *"How to Leave a Cult"* by Neil Gardner

- *"The Least of Gods Priorities"* by Bo Juel

- *"The Turning Sword"* by Parker Edwards

---

4. https://www.amazon.co.uk/s/ref=dp_byline_sr_book_2?ie=UTF8&text=Wolfgang+Herb-st&search-alias=books-uk&field-author=Wolfgang+Herbst&sort=relevancerank

Printed in Great Britain
by Amazon